A Message from Capital City Savings

On behalf of Capital City Savings I am ple... ...present *Kidmonton: True Stories of River City Kids*, which presents images of life in Edmonton through the years as experienced by its youngest citizens.

Credit unions have served the people of Edmonton for almost 70 years, providing them with the financial services and community support needed to build a great city. As Edmonton's centennial approached, we looked for a meaningful way to contribute to the celebrations in a manner that would honour the enduring values of the credit union system and Capital City Savings.

We believe this book accomplishes just that. At Capital City Savings, youth and the development of youth are one of our community investment priorities, as determined by our members and employees. We felt that the voice of youth should be represented during Edmonton's centennial, because they are part of our city's past and key to our future.

Community investment has always been a fundamental commitment of credit unions like Capital City Savings. We believe in sharing our success with the communities where our members and employees live and work.

In this spirit, Capital City Savings is proud to give youth a voice in this celebration of Edmonton's 100th anniversary. I hope you enjoy it.

Harry Buddle

Harry Buddle
President & CEO
Capital City Savings

Kidmonton

by Linda Goyette

TRUE STORIES OF RIVER CITY KIDS

BRINDLE
& GLASS

Library and Archives Canada Cataloguing in Publication
Goyette, Linda, 1955-
Kidmonton : true stories of River City kids / Linda Goyette.

ISBN 0-9732481-7-3

1. Edmonton (Alta.)—History—Juvenile literature. 2. Children—
Alberta—Edmonton—History—Juvenile literature. I. Title.

PS8613.O985K52 2004   j971.23'34   C2004-904674-8

Cover and interior images: Robert Nichols
Profile photographs are credited on page 115

🅢 CAPITAL CITY SAVINGS

The Edmonton Public Library gratefully acknowledges Capital City Savings and Credit Union's sponsorship of *Kidmonton*. We also wish to recognize the Department of Canadian Heritage, Canada Council for the Arts, Alberta Lottery Fund, Alberta Community Development, Alberta Foundation for the Arts, Alberta Historical Resources Foundation, the City of Edmonton Archives, the Office of the Mayor, the Clifford E. Lee Foundation and the Friends of the Edmonton Public Library in the development of all aspects of this centennial project. We appreciate the hard work and dedication of the many volunteers, including those who donated time, stories and funds to make the project possible. Working with Linda Goyette was a great pleasure.

 Canada Council   Conseil des Arts
for the Arts   du Canada

Brindle & Glass acknowledges the support of the Canada Council for the Arts and the Alberta Foundation for the Arts for our publishing program.

Brindle & Glass Publishing
www.brindleandglass.com

Brindle & Glass is committed to protecting the environment and to the responsible use of natural resources. This book is printed on 100% post-consumer recycled and ancient forest-friendly paper. For more information please visit www.oldgrowthfree.com.

1   2   3   4   5   07   06   05   04
PRINTED AND BOUND IN CANADA

to Evan, with love

The Stories

The First Ones

Do you like this place? We found it for you. On a winter day, more than eight thousand years before you were born, we followed rabbit tracks to the top of your highest hill, then slid down to the river's edge on frozen wolf hides.

We come from the north. Our people follow the herds to warmer places, always travelling. When the older ones stopped to make a camp, we slipped away into the snowy woods. No one saw us go. We chased a rabbit through the trees, and when it disappeared, we followed its tiny footprints to a clearing at the top of the hill. We looked down in surprise. Far below us a wide river twisted like a snake towards the sun.

We were hungry. Sliding down, down, down to the riverbank, we found a heavy stick and pounded a hole in the ice. We scooped the icy water into our cupped hands and took a drink. A silver-blue fish swam into the open space, and faster than a blink, my sister caught one tip of its tail and flipped the fish into the snow. We cooked it over a small fire, warming our hands in the wood smoke.

It began to snow, softly at first, and then heavily. The north wind bit the tips of our ears. Our eyelashes turned to icelashes. We squinted through the ice crystals, but soon we couldn't see our footprints along the shoreline, or our sliding place down the hill, because fresh snow covered every trace of our trail.

"We're lost," my sister whispered in a shivery voice. "We will disappear in the snow. Nobody will ever know we were here."

Did you know I carry the tooth of an ancient animal for good luck? I was told that if the tooth ever saved me from danger, I should hide it in a safe place for someone else. Would it help us today? I held the tooth in my closed fist, hoping it would lead us back through the blizzard to our clan.

"Keep walking," my sister said to me. "Don't stop."

We walked on the top of the snowdrift, counting how many steps we could take before our feet pushed through the snow's crust and we sank to our knees. We followed the river's edge. At last we heard a familiar voice, calling our names. Our grandmother was waving to us from the top of a cliff.

"Wait for us!" we shouted. We ran to meet her. She told us she'd been searching for us all day, and led us back to the fire.

This morning our family is moving on again. We've been walking since sunrise, deep into a ravine.

We buried the wild animal tooth for you to find near a creek that meets the river. When you touch it, remember we were the first human beings to taste this rushing water, cold and clean. Our names will be a secret. The river is our gift to you.

We Walked Across the Prairies

Tân'si! Are these the Beaver Hills? We need a rest.

We come from the east. Nine months ago we left our camp at York Factory near Hudson's Bay to travel with Attickasish and Connawapa and the English stranger called Henday. Our fathers are searching for western hunters who will trade beaver pelts to the Hudson's Bay Company. They are leading Henday because he doesn't know the territory.

Henday makes us laugh until our sides hurt. He is a tall man with shaggy hair and crooked teeth. He looks like a skinny bear with a long snout. At night in our tent he snores and whistles through his teeth in his sleep. When we tickle his bare feet with willow twigs, he wakes up with a snort and mutters funny words in his own language.

"Blathering Beelzebub!" he shouts into the darkness. "Blast of a blunderbuss!"

In the morning we ask him what these English words mean. He doesn't remember saying them.

Henday is trying hard to learn our language. He makes many silly mistakes when he tries to say our words. Once he grabbed his gun, and told our mother he was going hunting for *misisâhkwak* for us to eat the next day. "Don't hurry back," our mother said with a smile. *Misisâhkwak* means horseflies.

We travelled by canoe through the early summer. One night French-speaking traders sneaked into our camp on the river-bank, and shouted that Henday was a spy in their trading territory. There was a lot of yelling. They threatened to capture us, and send Henday to France! We ran for the woods, and hid in the highest branches of the poplar trees, listening to the shouts in three languages. Finally Henday convinced them to go away, and we crept from our hiding places.

The next day we were back on the river. When we reached the grassland, we left our canoes on the shore and began the long walk overland.

Have you ever walked across the prairies? We walked day after day, following rivers, through the summer and early fall. Yes, our feet hurt. Even so, we had a lot of fun, teaching Henday how to chase prairie dogs. "I've never seen these critters before," he said. "What funny little varmints."

That night Henday told us he was searching for the Archithinue people who live closer to the mountains.

"I'll promise them fine cloth, beads, and gunpowder if they will come to York Factory to trade their furs," he said.

Our mothers looked at each other without speaking. Finally Henday's wife said: "Why would they travel such a distance when they can trade with our people in this territory? Perhaps the Company will have to come here to trade with the Archithinue."

"To this wilderness?" he grumbled. "Impossible!"

We found the Archithinue at a camp with two hundred lodges. Henday told us that the chiefs offered him the pipe, and gave him buffalo tongue to eat. We stayed outside and traded our bows and hoops with the Archithinue of our own age. We ran races with them. They gave us a small pup as a gift when Attickasish said it was time for us to travel north.

The pup is never far from our heels as we walk. She chases chipmunks and magpies but sometimes we carry her when she's tired. All day we've pulled our sleds along the frozen Saskatchewan River, looking for a place to camp.

We hear soft laughter from the woods, as younger children of the Beaver Hills spy on us from behind the trees. "Don't worry about them," our brother said. "They're our relations. This is where our father was born."

Twelve of us will make our camp tonight where two rivers meet. We'll camp with the Beaver Hills people until the snow melts. Our fathers will build birch canoes for the journey to York Factory in the spring, and our mother will make snowshoes.

Henday promises we will have a feast for a saint named George at the end of *ayikîpîsim*, the frog moon. He says he will fly a cloth decorated with red, white, and blue sticks for his king. He asks us: "Are your bows ready? The geese are returning. I'd love to taste roast goose at the feast."

Maybe he knows that the kids in his camp are better hunters than him!

Every night Henday dips a feather into a pot of blue, and scratches words on a thin skin he calls paper. Our mother says he's telling the story of our journey here. We are *mihcet awâsisak*, the *nehiyawak*, of this territory. Did Henday tell you our names?

Jimmy Jock

Tell me about your horses. That's all I want to know about you.

How fast can you ride? How many horses do you own?

I'm Jimmy Jock Bird, and I can leap on a pony in one jump, and ride across the flats faster than riders twice my age. I work as an apprentice at Edmonton House, piling furs in the store-house after each trading day, but I don't plan to stay in this place like a rock beside the river. I want to ride into the mountains with Nicholas Montour, my uncle, and come back to tell my family about my hunting trips with the Kutenai and Salish tribes. I want to bring home new horses.

"Forget about going west," my father warned me yesterday. "You're going east, boy. I'm taking you to Mr. Geddes's school at York Factory this summer, since there is no school at Edmonton House. No arguments!"

Do you know why my father wants me to learn to read, write, and count in English? He is the boss for the Hudson's Bay Company in this part of Rupert's Land. He was born far away in England, so he gave English names to my brothers, and to me, and he called my mother "Mary," after his sister. Her true Cree name was Oomenahowish. She died when I was eight years old. Now I have a new stepmother, Elizabeth, from across the yard at Fort Augustus. At Edmonton House we speak Cree,

mixed with English and Gaelic and French.

Did you know our Cree name for Edmonton House is *Amiskwaciwâskahikan*?

I'm also learning the languages of all the trading peoples who come here. Arithmetic is the only language I don't want to learn. Who needs school? Any place without horses sounds like prison.

My friends and I race on horseback across the river flats. We want to be warriors on the plains, not clerks for the Company. We don't want to sit for long hours, drawing numbers on slates, in a place as cold and dreary as York Factory. We want to go hunting with the Montour family, and learn to drive the buffalo herds over the jumps.

"I can't believe how fast your children ride," Marie-Anne Gaboury Lagimodière tells my father. "They gallop at full speed without a saddle or bridle, only a loose rope around the horse's jaw. How does your son ride so fast without falling off?"

She doesn't know that I understand every word she says in French—not just *bonjour* or *votre petit garçon*.

My father grumbles that we should be working at our age, not racing. "Jimmy Jock is already eleven!" he says. Still he listens when visitors like Marie-Anne tell him that children at Fort Augustus and Edmonton House are famous for their love of horses and fine riding.

Have you seen the territory beyond our river, beyond the mountains? I'll ride there someday. What is it like?

The Hidden Boys

You will never know my name. My disappearance from your river valley will always be a mystery.

My people came to the Big House to trade beaver pelts and buffalo robes for hunting guns, knives, axes, copper pots, tobacco, and glass beads as small as seeds. You call us the Blackfoot people. We call ourselves *nitsitapii*.

Watching in all directions for our enemies, I waited on the south shore of your riverbank until the flag rose above Edmonton House. I held my ears when the cannon boomed. Our chief and the hunters crossed the river, and entered the gates for the pipe ceremonies, the speeches, and an exchange of gifts to honour the trade. We followed behind.

"I'll leave you here for a short time so you can learn the languages of these people," my grandfather told me. "Don't worry. I'll send some hunters to come and get you when they return to trade. Don't forget us."

I watched him turn away. I was a bit scared of this new place. Near the swimming hole I found an orphan boy who spoke my language. He'd stayed behind in the fort when his family died of smallpox, and he was happy to find a new brother.

The strangers fed us, and dressed us in their heavy clothes. The boss of this place is Iron Shirt, the man called John Rowand.

His nephews taught us their Cree language, and showed us their favourite places to hide in sandy caves near the riverbank. They wanted us to stay forever, but I was homesick. I waited for my grandfather to keep his promise.

One morning a familiar hunter arrived to trade, and he told me a secret with his eyes. The time had come. We were going home, but how? The people at Edmonton House had adopted my brother and me, and they thought we were better off with them.

"Stay close to me," I said to my new brother. The young hunter approached us, and knelt down to give my brother a blanket. "When I give the signal, run to our horses," he whispered in our language "Cover your heads with this."

We waited beside the stockade, holding the folded blanket. Suddenly we heard the call of a bird. Without looking over our shoulders, we scrambled toward the horses. Another hunter was waiting to lift us to our hiding place.

Through a day and night the strangers at the Big House searched for us in every room, under every pile of furs. "We watched the gate closely," the trading men told Iron Shirt's wife in Cree. "How could the boys have vanished?"

We rode away under their noses, hidden in saddlebags. This morning we are galloping south, laughing at the way we fooled them.

Victoria's Promise

My name is Victoria, like the faraway queen. I am thirteen years old, but I plan to live to be 105. That's a promise.

This is my first buffalo hunt. The families at Lac Ste. Anne chose the exact day of our departure in their council. They elected a leader, ten captains, and fifteen soldiers on horseback to guard us on the plains and keep our law in the camp. My father repaired and packed three Red River carts for our family.

We left our cabin after the leaves were out on the poplar trees, and our gardens were planted. Our leader, Ladouceur, tied a flag to his Red River cart, and waved his arm as a signal to all of us. The Métis of St. Albert and Fort Edmonton joined us along the way. We were one hundred families when we crossed the North Saskatchewan river below the Hudson's Bay fort. Our horses had to pull our carts across the river, and I was sure our cart would tip into the water and I'd drown. My brother Alexis could see how scared I was. "Don't worry," he said. "Don't you know how many times our horses have crossed this river before? They know the way."

We rode south past the tipis of the Papaschase band at the Two Hills. When we reached the Bear Hills I began to watch the horizon for the cloud of dust of a buffalo herd. I tried to listen for the thunder sound of their hoofs on the prairie. "You're

watching too soon," my mother said. "Ladouceur tells us we'll have to travel a long way to find the buffalo this year. We'll be lucky to find any at all."

My mother is a medicine woman. As we ride along, she tells me exactly what I will have to do to help her. Sometimes, at the wildest moment of the hunt, buffalo will charge the horses, and throw the riders. My mother sets the hunters' broken bones, and gives them highbush cranberries and willow bark so they can ride the next day without pain. She will also help Mrs. Courtepatte when it's time for her baby to be born.

The older boys in the Letendre, Campion, and Loyer families ride ahead as scouts to watch out for enemies. This morning I caught side of the first herd, a solid, moving mass in the distance. The riders of the chase jumped on their horses, with their guns and gunpowder horns, and raced toward the herd.

When the hunt is over, I'll go with the other women to bring the buffalo meat back to the camp. The older women will slice the meat carefully, and hang it on rails to smoke over a low fire. My job is to keep a little smoke going all day, and to help mix the saskatoon berries to make pemmican. We sew the pemmican into large bundles so heavy that two men are needed to lift each bundle into the cart. On top of the pemmican we pack the hides. We use every part of the buffalo except the horns, hoofs, and bones.

After a day's hard work I look forward to some fun in the evening. We camp in a circle of tipis beside the water. We have storytelling, horse races, games, and fiddle music in our camp.

This is the happiest time of the year for everyone in my family, but I wonder how long it will last?

My mother says the plains around Fort Edmonton were black with buffalo when she was thirteen. Now we travel farther south each spring to meet the herds, and every year they are harder to find.

Do you hunt buffalo in your time? Do you listen to the creaking and squeaking of wooden wheels as your carts turn toward home? I plan to live long enough to find out.

Annie Laurie's Moose Ride

I am still trying to decide why my life has been so unusual since I came to the North West Territories. Nothing is ho-hum in this place.

I've lived outside Fort Edmonton for only a few months, but I know all families in this tiny settlement. This morning Matt McCauley Jr. knocked on the door and asked if I'd like to go sliding on the hill behind his place.

"I have no sled, and no toboggan," I said.

Matt wasn't worried about that. "We make our own sleds here out of barrel staves," he said. "We have an extra one for you."

We pulled our barrel sleds through snowdrifts until we found a perfect, slippery place at the top of a steep hill. Soon we were flying toward the river. We cut sticks in the woods, and played shinny on the thick ice. Looking down I could see sturgeon swimming beneath my feet.

"I'm cold," I told Matt. "You keep sliding, and I'll walk up the hill on my way home."

He waved goodbye, and I began the long climb to our cabin. Can you imagine how surprised I was when I saw two moose looking straight down at me?

The moose were harnessed to a low sled of their own.

17

Behind them I recognized the young man who lives down the river from us. He delivers the mail every Saturday from Fort Edmonton to St. Albert.

"Would you like a ride to the top of the hill, Annie?" he asked.

I would, and I did!

The freighter said he had caught the moose in the ravine when they were young, and trained them to pull his mail sled. It looks something like a toboggan with a shoe-shaped animal-hide covering on top. I crawled inside. I felt cozy and comfortable with the mailbags as pillows around me. I was warm enough, too, with my hands in muff of white rabbit fur, and an old buffalo robe over my knees.

Standing behind me, the driver gave a shout and the two moose pulled us to the top of the hill. My parents said I could go along for the ride out the St. Albert Trail. We delivered the mail to a few houses along the way. On the way home we stopped at the Norris halfway house for stew, bannock, and hot tea. The sled driver gave a bag of candy to every child at Mr. Norris's house, and we played hide-and-seek together in the barn.

I think I'm going to like Edmonton. I can snare rabbits with my brother. I can play shinny on the ice. I can ride my pony to school. Best of all, I can glide along the St. Albert Trail in a moose-drawn sled.

What do you do for fun on a Saturday afternoon in winter?

Billy's Trick

Rumours are flying around here, and the grownups are losing their wits.

They're afraid that a big war is coming our way. The Métis and Cree to the east along the river are rising up in a rebellion. They say Canada has no right to claim their territory.

My parents think I'm too young to understand, so they whisper in the kitchen late at night. I hear every word from my hiding place behind the woodstove.

I live in Fort Saskatchewan at the headquarters of the North West Mounted Police. My father is the commander of the police fort, so he's responsible for keeping everyone safe in Fort Edmonton, St. Albert, Lac Ste. Anne, and the district in between. My mother is responsible for keeping me safe.

"No pranks, right now, Billy," she tells me every morning. "I don't have a spare moment to deal with your shenanigans."

Do you know why she's rattled? Yesterday a settler from Fort Saskatchewan hitched up his horses to a wagon, and rode into Fort Edmonton at top speed. "They've captured the police fort, and massacred the police!" he told the crowd.

It wasn't true, of course. Father and I were eating porridge in perfect health at the time. Everyone else in Fort Saskatchewan was fine, too.

"What a fool!" my father said, when he found out about the big scare in Edmonton. "I have half a mind to lock up that ninny in the barracks."

Nothing bad has happened here, but I heard my father whisper that his men had searched every tipi in Bobtail's camp. The chief was so insulted he seized my father's horse by the bridle. My father pulled his revolver. The Cree men pulled out their rifles. Nobody fired a shot, but my father says he locked up six young Cree men in the guardroom, not far from where I sleep. "We've got Lawrence Garneau, too," he whispered to my mother.

Who is Garneau? Nobody tells me anything.

I feel like starting a Northwest Rebellion of my own. Father shouts orders. Mother rolls bandages and loads shotgun shells. Everybody around here is jumpy, and nobody pays attention to me.

Sometimes I get even. Last night I tied a sleigh bell to my black tomcat, and gently pushed him outside the gate.

The guard on duty caught sight of a dangerous intruder creeping along the palisades.

"Stop right there, or I'll shoot!" the guard shouted.

The intruder scurried towards him. The guard lifted up his rifle and shot a warning blast into the air. The noise woke up all the policemen in the Fort. They ran helter-skelter towards the palisades, waving their shotguns, and hollering warnings. They looked so funny in their long underwear.

"Take cover!" the guard yelled to them from above. "I see hundreds of warriors approaching the Fort."

My mother must have heard me giggle. She grabbed me by the scruff of my collar, and told me she'd lock me in the guard-house herself if I didn't behave.

A black tomcat sauntered into the Fort, jingling all the way.

Eliza's Treaty

You live near the place where I was born. You travel on the same trail that I walked one summer day with my family and all of our belongings.

You follow Eliza Papastew Gladue's footsteps even if you don't know it.

Eliza, that's me. I want to tell you about my moving day on August 12, 1887. I was seven years old. I'm ten now, but I can still remember every minute of that day.

I woke up in our summer lodge, listening to the summer rain falling on the poplar trees, and waiting for my mother to call for me. "Please stay close by today," she said, as she handed me a cup of tea and some bannock to eat. "I'll need your help."

All morning I carried our clothing and blankets, our cooking pots and lanterns, to our cart. I carefully tucked my rag doll into a saddlebag so she wouldn't be lost in the confusion. I wrapped my ribbon dress in a blanket, too.

Around us the other families were loading everything they owned on carts and packhorses. La Louise and her four boys. Cahcoosis and Onachees. Napasis and her children. Mrs. Duquette and her son. Cecile and her children. Wahwaskasee and his family. Everyone.

"Here is the garden hoe I borrowed from you, Lucie," said

Cecile, walking toward my mother. "Where will you be going?"

I didn't wait to hear my mother's answer. Instead I walked to our winter cabin, a place we only used for a few cold months each year. In a dark corner I found an old kettle. When I touched its wooden handle, I remembered holding a cup of hot tea beside a fire on cold winter nights. Maggie and Kaytaygan would tell me stories about how they danced at Fort Edmonton when they were young and beautiful. "Did you kiss the chief factor on New Year's Day?" I would ask. "Did you win the women's races?" They always said yes.

Thinking about them, I swept the floor. I picked up the kettle and closed the cabin door.

Have you ever moved away from your first home? Then you know how strange I felt that morning.

I was born three years after my father, Chief Papastayo, signed Treaty 6 papers along with the other chiefs from around Fort Edmonton. My mother told me I appeared in the hungriest year, after the buffalo disappeared, and we had very little to eat all winter. After that my father claimed our reserve on the south shore of the river, opposite Fort Edmonton, as part of the land promised to Cree people in the treaty. We had already camped there for many years.

My first memory is of the thirst dance on our Papaschase reserve when I was four. A man in our band invited hundreds of people to the celebration and the ceremonies after his daughter was cured of her illness. I was a little bit scared of all the strangers in our camp, but I remember my mother holding me up to meet all of my relations. My brothers and sisters took my cousins to cool their bare feet in our lake. That was a long time ago.

"Why are we leaving our reserve?" I asked my mother as I put the kettle on top of her stack of blankets. She was harnessing the old horse to our cart.

"You are too young to understand," she told me.

"Where are we going?"

"Most people will go to Enoch Lapotac's reserve, at least at first."

My mother took the reins, whistled to the old horse, and turned our cart towards the crossing place on the North Saskatchewan River. The water sparkled in the summer sunlight.

My father once told us that Treaty 6 would last as long as that river flowed.

Looking over my shoulder, I squeezed my mother's hand. "I don't know when," I whispered to her, "but we're coming back."

Our Raft Trip to a New Home

We travelled by raft on the river in a snowstorm. Have you ever done that?

We are the Yureichuks. We were born in a village in the Carpathian mountains in Galicia. One day our father came home to tell us we were leaving soon for Canada where farmland was free.

We crossed the Atlantic Ocean in the bottom of a huge ship, so seasick we could barely crawl out of our bunks. We travelled in a slow train across the empty country to Winnipeg, then Calgary, then north to the end of the railway tracks at Strathcona.

Our money was almost gone when we arrived here. All we had left was $7.50, and we needed it to buy food.

My father went with another Galician man to search for a homestead around Edmonton. They tramped all over the countryside for a week, hungry and tired, but the good land had been taken.

My mother waited behind with us in Strathcona. We slept in a stable until my father returned. "No land yet," he said. "I'm sorry."

We knew another family, our old friends from home, would help us, but their homestead was far away from Edmonton.

"I have an idea," said my father. He built a raft to take us east on the North Saskatchewan River. We rolled a heavy chest, full of our belongings, from the Strathcona stable down the street to the riverbank. A man stopped and loaded the chest on his wagon, then helped to roll it to the raft. Kids came running to watch us float away. We heard them mocking us. "Galicians, go homestead," they yelled. The wagon driver refused to take our money. He waved goodbye, shaking his head.

It was already afternoon when we shoved off from shore. The water was shallow, and the raft barely moved past John Walter's lumberyard. On the evening of the second day, we docked at Fort Saskatchewan. Some German settlers, who spoke our language, told us we would have to travel a week on the river to reach our destination. My father ran to the store and bought some potatoes, pork fat, and bread with the rest of our money.

On the raft we made a small fire inside a pan, baked potatoes, and smeared them with pork fat. This was our meal.

Next, my father built a small hut on the raft to shelter us from rain and an icy wind.

On the third night the blizzard began. Our raft hit a sandbar. My parents pulled off their boots and jumped in the water in their bare feet to push the raft forward. It wouldn't move. Our firewood was soaked, and we began to shiver. Our mother put a featherbed over us, and we huddled under frozen blankets and snow.

It is a miracle we didn't die that night. Early in the morning a Cree family crossing the river on horses rescued us. They carried our belongings, and us, to their cabin. We sipped hot tea and ate bannock, and we thawed out.

"You Galician?" the Cree man said with his few English words.

"I go homestead, Victoria settlement," our father said with his few English words.

The Cree father spread all of his fingers on both hands to explain the distance in miles to the nearest farm of a Galician. He pointed to a path that led up a hill. Our father whispered something to our mother, and squeezed her hand. He walked away.

We waited behind. Children our age tried to speak to us, but we couldn't understand their greetings.

"*Tân'si,*" they said, to say hello.

"*Dobry den,*" we said, to say hello, too.

Toward evening Steve Ratsoy came to fetch us. He picked up the baby in his strong arms, and we climbed into his wagon. We waved goodbye to the people who saved our lives, and we never saw them again.

A ship, a train, and a raft brought us to our new home. We remember our cold nights on the river, and the coyotes' howls.

1909
The Day the Edmonton Police
Banned Tobogganing

If you live in Edmonton you might know the steep hill on 106th Street downtown.

Do you call it Edgar Nobles's Hill? Probably not. It happens to be my favourite sledding hill, but I don't expect Edmonton will name a hill after a kid like me.

Until last week all of my friends at MacKay Avenue School loved to toboggan right down the middle of 106th Street at top speed. Sometimes we had a little trouble. One night Wop May's sister slammed her sled straight into a horses' hitching post, and broke her leg. Most of the time we just had fun. The coasting was best after supper in the dark.

The trouble is that Edmonton is growing in too much of a hurry. We have 18,500 people here now, and a few dozen automobiles. Have you ever noticed that Edmonton's drivers never watch where they're going? Some of them drive twenty miles an hour! Every day I see another automobile scaring the freighters' horses half to death.

We have streetcars in Edmonton, too. A ride costs a nickel. To celebrate the first streetcar ride, the city held a running contest. The conductors said all boys and girls who could run along beside the streetcar from Jasper Avenue, down 109th Street, along

33

97th Avenue, and over the Low Level Bridge, would get a free ride back to the north side of the river.

All of my friends tried to do it. I ran like the dickens, but I was out of breath before I reached the Low Level Bridge. I had to walk home with slush in my boots.

That blasted streetcar—and a seven-year-old boy—put a stop to our sledding on 106th Street.

I never did hear the kid's name. One day he raced down the middle of the street on his sled, across the streetcar tracks, right under a moving streetcar.

"That child had a guardian angel on the sled behind him," my aunt told my mother. How did she know?

Anyway, after that big scare the parents made a big fuss about children sledding in dangerous places. The police announced that the kids of Edmonton couldn't go coasting on 106th Street anymore. We had to keep our sleds off the streets, and on ordinary hills.

Tough luck for us. Where do you go coasting?

High Level Hijinks

The old folks say we will be sorry if we keep up this tomfoolery.

"Four men died building that bridge, and you'll be next!" they shout at us. "Get down from there!"

We don't always listen.

My name is Grace, and I am eight. I live just two blocks away from the new High Level Bridge: the eighth wonder of the world, and my favourite place in Edmonton.

I love the way the streetcars rattle, creak, and rumble their way across the High Level. Streetcars run on two tracks on the top of the bridge, and the train travels on a track in between. The lower level is for automobiles and people on foot.

I keep an eye out for pranksters. Once I saw a boy ride a donkey across the top of the bridge, leading a parade of laughing students.

Another student rode an automobile across the top. Older kids dare each other to ski along the railway tracks before the train whistle blows. Student nurses drop their ugly training shoes off the bridge to celebrate graduation.

One morning two boys tied their toboggan to the back of the streetcar to hitch a ride to the sledding hills on the north side. The streetcar sped up! The boys gripped the toboggan ropes in terror as they swayed from side to side. They could see over the edge of

the bridge with each outswing—and there is no railing!

Finally they managed to roll off the toboggan, and lie perfectly still on the streetcar track until they stopped shaking. Then they crawled across the bridge on their bellies, pulling their toboggan behind them. Never try this! They are still shaking.

My little sister, Frances, got into trouble on the High Level Bridge, too.

Frances is three years old. She tried to cross the top of the bridge with her four-year-old friend.

Unfortunately for Frances, Father happened to be driving to work downtown when he spied them up above. He slammed on the brakes, and ran to catch the two runaways.

Frances isn't one bit sorry. "Keep an eye on her, Grace," said my mother. "I'm sure she'll do it again!"

The other day Father and I were riding the streetcar over the High Level Bridge when something went wrong. We stopped with a terrible jerk.

"Everybody off!" the conductor ordered.

"Are you out of your blooming mind, sir?" an old woman yelled from the back. She folded her arms, and refused to budge.

Father told me we couldn't sit there all day. He held my hand tightly as we walked along the train tracks.

"Don't look down," he whispered, but I couldn't help myself.

I squinted through the open spaces at the automobiles, trees and the cold river below. I could see the old Hudson's Bay fort on the north shore. My knees wobbled and buckled with each step. It was the finest fright I've ever experienced.

Fred's Flood

My name is Fred, but would you like to call me Noah? I survived Edmonton's Great Flood of 1915. More than once, as a matter of fact.

My friends and I were playing on the riverbank when the rain started. We dug a cave to bury some treasure that I won't tell you about. We had our backs to the river, so we didn't see it rising.

On Monday morning our dugout disappeared under the floodwater.

Have you ever heard our river roar like that? All day I raced along the top of McDougall Hill, back and forth, watching the river spill over the riverbank. Every kid in Edmonton searched for the highest, best place to watch the flood.

We saw families down on the Flats pack their belongings on trucks in the biggest hurry of their lives. Little kids waved up to us from rescue canoes. Jenny Slidinsky's dad in Riverdale chained their house to a tree, but the floodwater swept away sixty other houses.

Everything floated by us—homes, uprooted trees and logs, lumber, even stranded cows and chickens on rooftops—and a huge mess piled up against the Low Level Bridge.

"That bridge will collapse for sure," said my pal, but he was wrong.

At noon the Canadian Northern Railway sent a train with two locomotives to weigh down the bridge so we wouldn't lose it, too. The plan worked. A huge stable from John Walter's place crashed into the bridge railings, but the Low Level Bridge stayed put.

Grownups were in a big panic, as usual. Everybody tried to help out with the rescues, and the emergency shelters, but so many men are away at war right now that the volunteers were soon exhausted. Coal miners set dynamite charges to break up the dangerous log jam below the bridge. Water flooded about seven hundred houses on the Flats, covering walls, floors, and ceilings with slick, slimy mud.

At 10 o'clock on Monday night you couldn't see a flicker of light in Edmonton. The river flooded the Rossdale Power Plant, and our electricity went out. We had no drinking water for a long while, either.

The flood wasn't a complete disaster. Okay, I'll admit it. I had fun. My buddies and I went down to the Flats, pulled up what was left of the wooden sidewalks, and made rafts. We were the Huckleberry Finns of Edmonton, Alberta.

Floating down the street rivers, we would pull ourselves in front of a house, then holler for help. What a commotion! People hurried from all directions to rescue us. Then we'd pull our raft around a corner, float along a new street, and try the same stunt again.

We spent all day getting rescued!

Alfred's Letter

My world is upside down. Nothing is right.

What did people in Edmonton do to deserve this stupid war?

"Stick to Alberta, and be an Albertan, and then it won't be your business whether Serbia or Bulgaria becomes larger," Dad told me in a letter from the other side of the Atlantic Ocean. The war seemed so far away then.

My mother keeps his letters in a special box. "They're precious to us," she says quietly. "We'll keep them."

My father wrote to each one of us—me, William, Laura, Dorothy and Gladys—taking turns so nobody would feel left out. He told us interesting stories about his life as a soldier in the trenches, and he asked questions about everything at home.

"If I don't come back, you will be more or less left in charge of your younger brothers and sisters," he wrote to me, because I am the eldest. "That will mean that you must help them, and when they make mistakes you must try to put them right."

I'm only fifteen. I'm not ready to be a father.

I remember how proud I was of my father last year. When our hero Griesbach came back to Edmonton to recruit the 49th Battalion, the posters on Jasper Avenue said: "The present war is the Greatest War in History." My father was old enough to avoid

the war, or be an officer, but he'd already joined up as a regular soldier in the army.

My little sister Gladys was at MacKay Avenue School the day we received the terrible news. The teacher told her that our father had been killed, and she was to go straight home.

She walked home by herself. Why did that have to happen? I could have walked to meet her. I didn't know.

I wonder what happened to our letters to Dad? Dorothy sent clippings from the *Edmonton Bulletin* and *The Edmonton Journal* about the big flood. William sent his arithmetic homework, and asked for help with long division. We sent Valentines and Christmas cards, too. Were our letters lost in the mud?

I mailed my last letter to my father on April 2, 1916. I told him about my role in a play at Victoria School.

My letter came back to me unopened from a war hospital in France. Someone at the hospital stamped an ugly, black word on the envelope. "Deceased," it said. The word means dead.

I will stick to Alberta, Dad. I will take your place.

Gertrude and the Castle

Every kid in Edmonton knows about the castle on the hill. My father is the king of the castle.

The castle, of course, is the Hotel Macdonald. The Mac opened in 1915, and people in Edmonton love the grand place, even if they never go inside the big front door. The Prince of Wales danced in the ballroom with Edmonton's prettiest girls. I plan to dance with the prince myself on his next visit. "Prince Edward, I have a question to ask you," I will say, as he twirls me around the dance floor. "Is Buckingham Palace as grand as our palace on Jasper Avenue?"

The Mac is extra-special to me because it brought my family to Edmonton. My father, Rudolph Jacob, is the hotel's first pastry chef. He can make all kinds of mouth-watering desserts, and everyone says he creates the finest chocolate éclairs in Alberta.

He leaves our house on 95th Street and 103rd Avenue very early in the morning to walk to work. I like to visit him later in the day. Do you ever go exploring at the Mac? Look for my secret ramp to the old kitchen, the entrance where the delivery boys bring fresh fruit, vegetables, and meat from the city's grocers and butchers near Market Square.

My father will accept only the finest ingredients for his

three-layer lemon cakes, apple tarts, delicate sugar cookies, and blueberry pies. He always wears a long white apron and a high chef's hat, perfectly clean, without a spot of chocolate on his shirt. I don't know how he does it.

"I'm very busy right now, Gertrude," he says, stirring the sauces and sifting the flour. "You can only stay for a minute." He dips his wooden spoon into the chocolate sauce, closes his eyes, and tastes it to be sure it's perfect. I wonder why he always closes his eyes when he tastes his creations? Then he puts down the spoon, and gives me a treat to eat on the way home.

"*Auf wiedersehen,*" he whispers as he puts a gingersnap in my pocket.

We have two languages in our family. We speak English outside the house, and German at home. My parents were born in Germany but they met in New York—in a German bakery, of course, where my mother, Maria, worked. You could say it was a delicious romance. A few years later they got married and brought their best recipes to western Canada. They travelled across the Prairies on the train with all the other chefs and cooks who found jobs at the Hotel Macdonald. I always feel lucky to come home from school to a plate of warm cookies on the kitchen table.

One Christmas my father decided to surprise the people of Edmonton with a sweet holiday treat from Germany. Leaning over his baking table, he melted sugar to make tiny houses and churches, shops, and clock towers. He worked all day on his creation. When he was finished he put tiny cinnamon hearts on the houses for chimneys, lemon drops for windows, and vanilla icing on the rooftops for snow. The Christmas village was made entirely of sugar, a magical town that glistened in the candlelight.

Hundreds of people came to the Mac to admire his display.

"What will Rudolph think of next?" the hotel manager said to every visitor. "He has a gift for making the people of this city happy."

A few nights after Christmas, my father called my mother from the lobby of the Mac. He told her he was bringing home a delicious surprise for us. "Tell the children to wait at the door," he said. We couldn't believe our eyes when we saw him carrying a large silver tray up the front steps. He had brought home the sugar village, just for us.

"You will be the only people in Edmonton who will be allowed to taste it," he said to us in German. "Enjoy every little bit of it." And so we did.

Next Christmas I think my father should build a gingerbread castle that looks exactly like the Mac. I've already imagined it. The castle could stand on a hill of vanilla ice cream, high above a curving river of ice-blue peppermints. Beyond the front door, red licorice streetcars could travel along a jelly-bean Jasper Avenue. The streetlights could be candy canes. The hotel doorman could be a chocolate soldier. My father could put a butterscotch ghost in the highest window of the castle, but I would eat it up before it had a chance to frighten anyone.

Do you believe that ghosts haunt the Mac? I can tell you one thing. As long as my father is the pastry chef, they will never be hungry ghosts.

Peace In Flight

Will he fly overhead today? I climb out of my bedroom window, and sit on the sloping roof of our house, looking up at the sky. My father says roof-sitting is against the law in Edmonton. Do I give a hoot? I'm waiting for somebody important.

My name is Peace, but that's not because I'm peaceful. My parents named me after the river up north. I live with my family in a big, comfortable house at the end of Villa Avenue, on the edge of the Groat Ravine, in Edmonton, Alberta, the Dominion of Canada, British Empire, Planet Earth, Milky Way, Universe.

I'm not boasting, but I've flown in a real aeroplane with Edmonton's famous pilot Wop May. He gave us a ride as a favour to my parents.

I loved it! From the sky we looked down at the tiny specks of the Cloverdale kids swimming in the river. We asked Wop to swoop under the High Level Bridge, like he did before the baseball game at the Exhibition.

"I'd better not try that again with young passengers," he said. "Your parents might be mad at me."

High over Jasper Avenue we pretended we were escaping the Red Baron, just like Wop did in the war. Our friends from Glenora School stood in their yards, far below, waiting for us.

We dived low over their houses. They waved and whooped

and yelled from below.

After we landed Wop told me that every time he flew over our house he'd wave with three gloved fingers as a secret signal to my family and me.

I am waiting this morning for the rumble of an aeroplane.

"Hurry up!" my sister Norah is calling from the yard below.

Today is Saturday. This morning we've decided to follow my brother to his secret hideout in the deepest gully of the ravine. We'll hike the old trail along the creek to the river. For lunch we'll roll potatoes in birch bark, and roast them over a campfire.

Last winter we found a cave near my brother's fort. I told my sister I saw a bear in this hiding place—a tall tale, I'll admit. There are no bears in Edmonton anymore. On a dare Norah pushed through the saskatoon bushes to explore the dark cave. She must have seen a shadow, or maybe it was a hobo cooking his dinner in a dry place. She shrieked so loudly that we both ran up the hill and left our toboggan in the deep snow.

Norah told everyone at school the next day that she had definitely seen the front paws of a Rocky Mountain grizzly in the Groat Ravine. Mind you, I told my friends that Wop May taught me how to fly an aeroplane in a loopty-loop, backwards, with my eyes closed. My grandmother says I should keep my feet on the ground.

Norah is shouting again from the yard, waving up at me.

"Time to go!" she hollers.

"Wait one more minute!" I yell back.

I search every corner of Canada's bluest sky . . . hoping.

Odilé's New Shoes

Do you like my beautiful shoes? I've owned them for exactly one day.

My old shoes lost their shine in Edmonton. When I walked they pinched my toes. The heels were worn flat, and you could see my socks through the splits in the shabby leather. "You need to take care of them," my mother used to say, but I did take care of them. I was seven when I got them, and now I'm nine. My old shoes died of old age.

Last summer we piled everything we owned on a neighbour's truck, and rode into the city. My mother didn't look over her shoulder at our farm. "In Edmonton," my father told her, "everything will be better."

My Dad found a job cutting meat at the Burns packing plant, but he cut his hand and had to quit. He tried barbering, but discovered that people cut their own hair in hard times. He found a job at a mine in Coal Valley, but he was laid off and we had to come back to the city when we went broke.

My father walks the soles off his own shoes, looking for work.

"Your Dad's on relief," say the teasing kids in the schoolyard.

Their shoes look no better. Lots of kids go barefoot in the summer. In the winter some wear old moccasins, with rubber

boots pulled over them, and rubber rings from sealer jars around their ankles so they don't fall off. Did you think I was the only one with old shoes? I wasn't.

A girl fainted in my class one morning. Miss Hanley shook her by the shoulder, and asked her what she'd had eaten for breakfast. The girl answered: "It wasn't my turn."

We have enough to eat at our house. My parents raise chickens, and sell vegetables from their garden plots. My job is to go door-to-door selling the eggs for twenty-five cents a dozen. Sometimes I get a nickel tip and I buy a Macintosh Toffee bar, my favourite. Sometimes I go to the Dreamland Theatre on Jasper to see a Shirley Temple movie.

City kids find lots of ways to make a nickel. Some go the dump on Grierson Hill, find old wheels, and make wagons. Then they pull their wagons behind the big stores, and through the downtown alleys, looking for wooden crates. They break up the crates and sell the wood as kindling at Market Square.

We have lots of fun, no matter what happens. Yesterday we had a Christmas tree and treats in our class. Miss Hanley announced a surprise contest.

"Write down a number, and your name on piece of paper," she said, "and put it in my hat. The winner will receive a present. If you win, you can't open the parcel until you get home."

I carefully wrote my name, and the number "seven," then raced to the teacher's desk to put my scrap of paper in her blue hat.

We all held our breath, and waited. Miss Hanley picked up

her hat. "Odilé," she said, holding up a piece of paper over her head. "You win!"

At home I opened the box to find a new pair of shoes.

Thank you, Miss Hanley. I know what you did.

Peter's War

Are you like me? Did you move to Edmonton as a stranger from a faraway country?

I am trying to learn to speak English by practicing the sound of my new name. I was born Peter Offenbacher. In Edmonton I will be known as Peter Owen. I am starting my life again.

When I was eight years old in Germany, the new Nazi government began to mistreat Jewish families like mine for no reason at all. My parents were desperate to send their children away from danger, so they were relieved when strangers in Edmonton offered to help.

Harry and Frances Friedman had never met me, or my parents, but they worked hard to save my life. They never gave up on me.

The Friedmans asked the Canadian government for permission to bring me to Edmonton. At first Canada refused. Government officials said the country had no more room for European refugees like me.

For one long year, Mr. Friedman pleaded and coaxed and argued with stubborn people in many letters to Ottawa. He told them I was just thirteen years old, and in danger. He said his family in Edmonton would pay all of my expenses.

"The boy is related to intimate friends of mine," he said in

one letter to Ottawa. "I am reliably informed he is a healthy, bright lad with a promising future, if given half a chance."

The government must have been tired of receiving so many letters from Edmonton. They told Mr. Friedman he could bring me across the ocean if he paid one thousand dollars for the safety and security of the Canadian people.

What did they think I was going to do wrong? Blow up the High Level Bridge?

My situation in Germany was becoming more dangerous. One day I rode home from school on my bicycle, and passed the synagogue where I'd had my bar mitzvah. I was shocked to see only ashes and ruins where the building used to be. I saw an old man on the street with an angry crowd screaming at him. When I reached home, I found out the Nazis had arrested my uncle although he always obeyed the law.

Soon after, almost like magic, I received permission to come to Edmonton.

I travelled halfway around the world all by myself. I had no parents or other grownups with me to keep me company.

I arrived at the CNR Station in Edmonton with nothing much in my suitcase. It was very cold outside. I miss my family but the Friedmans are treating me very well. They hired a reporter from *The Edmonton Journal* to teach me to speak English. Every afternoon I meet him for lessons on the balcony at the Hotel Macdonald.

The students in my class treat this war as a kind of game. They have snowball fights with the American soldiers who are stationed all over the city. They boast about older brothers who are pilots high over Blatchford Field, and older sisters who are fixing warplanes at Aircraft Repair.

Their war doesn't hurt. Not yet, anyway. They have never heard hateful shouts, marching boots, or smashing glass on Jasper Avenue. They have never been afraid of a knock on the door.

Do you know the best thing about Edmonton? We are safe here.

Attention! It's Time to Mention Our Inventions!

Edmonton kids are great inventors. I guess kids in Calgary or Saskatoon or Winnipeg make some of the same things, but our stuff works better. That's a plain Canadian fact.

I've drawn a few sketches of our inventions to let you in on our trade secrets. That's my signature at the bottom: Bob Davies. I live at 9525 109th Avenue, and my friend Ernie lives two houses down. We hang around all summer with a gang of kids, forgetting about teachers, and having as much fun as possible before September sends us back to Norwood School.

We make things and we go places all summer without anybody worrying about us. In the hot afternoons we might make a racecar for the soap box derby on McDougall Hill. We fix the steering wheel so the car can make the sharp left turn at the finish-line barricades. We do that for a while, and then we make model airplanes out of balsa wood.

Sometimes we take empty jars to the Pioneer Manufacturing plant on 108A Avenue, and get the workers to fill up the jar with creamy peanut butter for a quarter. Then we sit at the open back door of the factory in case any peanuts spill off the conveyor belt and bounce our way. If we're noisy enough, the factory workers pay us in peanuts to get lost.

After that we might sneak under the fence at Clarke Stadium to play a football game; or walk to the Gyro Park on 95th Street to swing on double-crossed chains around metal maypoles; or scrounge some money from somebody's sister to go the Edmonton Exhibition. We might hike to the Borden Park Zoo to make weird faces at the monkeys, and to growl at the bear in the bear pit. We might go for a swim in the Borden Park pool.

After that we might hike through the yard of the Capital City Box Factory—some bigger kids go joy-riding on the little railway cars—and then cross the train tracks, and run down Lovers' Lane trail in Kinnaird Ravine. We search for rabbits and garter snakes in the woods. Then we climb the hill to the sand hoodoos overlooking the river, and build a high fort to spy on the Riverdale kids who are fishing down below.

All that happens before supper.

Back home we eat as quickly as possible and go outside again. All down the block you can hear screen doors slamming, and mothers calling: "Be back before dark!"

After supper, all along 109th Avenue, a big crowd of kids gets together to play Run Sheep Run, Kick the Can, Can Cricket, Hide and Seek, and other games until it gets dark. It's a good thing there aren't too many cars in Edmonton. We run straight across the avenue, up the streets, and across the back lanes, without thinking about cars and trucks.

As soon as the sun goes down, and we forget to go home, we raid the gardens between 92nd Street and the Stadium. We race back to our headquarters for a feast of raw carrots. (We rub off the dirt first, of course.) Sometimes we roast borrowed potatoes in a bonfire in the Riddles' backyard until the potato skins are crispy and the insides are steaming hot. This is just delicious if somebody remembers to borrow a salt shaker.

The next morning I sit on the front steps with Ernie. We try to think of something new to do.

"What do you wanna do?" I say to Ernie. "It sure is hot today."

"I dunno Bob, what do you wanna do?" he says to me. "It sure is hot."

We say this, back and forth a few times, as neighbourhood girls jump rope on the sidewalk. They yell skipping rhymes until we get a headache. "All in TOGETHER girls, we are the WEATHER girls. Tell us WHEN your birthday IS! January, FEBRUARY . . . "

Pretty soon Ernie is annoyed and bored, and I am, too, so we decide to make something. Here's a short list of our Edmonton inventions, with instructions in case you want to try them.

Kites: Take two thin strips of wood. Bind them together in a T-shape with string. Tie string around the outer frame. Fold newspaper over the string and wood frame. [*The Edmonton Journal* works just as well as the *Edmonton Bulletin*.] Make a string tail, and tie bows of cloth or newspaper to the tail. Tie a long length of string around a large spool, or wood block, and attach to the kite. Go to the Gyro playground, or the Hudson's Bay Reserve, and get Ernie to run as fast as he can across the field. The kite almost never flies, but it's really fun to make.

Wallpaper twirling: Find the remainders of two old rolls of wallpaper. Attach a wooden, spring-loaded clothespin to one end of the roll, tie a long string to the clothespin, and then play this ribbon-twirling game while running. The purpose of the game is to make the wallpaper twirl out without stepping on it, or letting it rip. This game has no rules, and no real point, but it beats skipping.

Stilts: Find old two old boards, and nail small blocks of wood near the bottom end on each one. To get on the darn things without falling, I stand on the front steps and climb on one stilt at a time while Ernie holds the stilts. Then I lean against the steps on my stilts, and bend down, and hold Ernie's stilts as he tries to climb on. Then we both fall down. Eventually we walk along the back lanes, and spy on gardens that might be good for a raid after dark.

Summer Scooter: Find an old pair of metal roller skates. Use the skate-tightening key as a screwdriver to separate each skate into two sections: the toe section and the heel section. Nail the two sections underneath a two-by-four board, one at each end. Find a wooden apple box. Nail it to the front end of the board. Find an old broken hockey stick, and break it into two sections. Nail the hockey stick bits to the top of the apple box as scooter handles. Nail a coffee tin or a tobacco tin to the front of the apple box, and put a candle inside, to make a headlight. (Be prepared. The candle goes out.) Race other kids on scooters along sidewalks. You can make wagons for little kids out of apple boxes, too.

Snow Scooter: After the first snowfall in September or October, take the summer scooter and unscrew the roller skate wheels. Put the wheels away in the garden shed until next summer. Nail the apple box, with the hockey stick handles and the coffee-can headlight, to the top of a broken wooden sled. The snow scooter doesn't work in deep, fresh snow, but it is good for racing on hard-packed snow in very cold weather. Run and push the sled to get going, and then jump on for a bit of a glide.

What do you make for fun? Are your inventions as good as mine?

Hockey Hero of 65th Street

Here's an Edmonton riddle for you. What kind of hockey player has no skates, no puck, no shin pads, no hockey gloves, no indoor arena, and a bright future in the NHL?

Stumped? The answer is Johnny Bucyk. That's me.

I play street hockey in my rubber boots from October to April, day after day, night after night. Okay, don't laugh. My buddies and I use kitchen brooms for hockey sticks. We roll up *Maclean's* magazines, or old Eaton's catalogues, and shove them under our wool pants for shin pads. We wear homemade wool mitts instead of hockey gloves—even the goalie—and we wear earmuffs or toques, not helmets.

I knew you'd ask about the pucks. Well, how can I put this politely? Sometimes we use old softballs and tennis balls, but in an emergency, we follow the milk wagons as they make deliveries through North Edmonton. Did you know that horses are hockey fans? The horses that pull milk wagons kindly drop their manure near the corner of 65th Street and 129th Avenue. We wait until it freezes solid, and then, wham! He shoots, he scores!

We don't have organized teams like you do. We have disorganized teams. Any kid who happens to show up on our street corner can play for free. We have no coaches, no uniforms, and no rules or regulations except the ones we make up ourselves.

Every game goes into overtime, not because the game is tied, but because we never want to quit playing and go home. The city is our rink.

School is torture in Edmonton in wintertime.

All morning we sit in our wooden desks, and watch the hands of the clock move toward noon. Tick . . . tick . . . tick. King George stares down at us from his picture frame on the wall above the blackboard. You can tell from his eyes he feels sorry for us. Our sweaters are scratchy and hot. The radiator hisses. The teacher's chalk screeches across the blackboard, sending shivers up our spines. We wait forever, then suddenly it's lunchtime, and we're out the door before you can spell Fort Saskatchewan backwards.

"You boys will freeze your ears out there!" the teacher shouts behind us. "Put your hats on! It's thirty-five below, and the wind is howling!"

We ignore her, of course. We find a smooth, slippery part of the street where it hasn't been sanded. I scrape the ice and that's our rink.

After our lunch, our waiting game goes into triple overtime.

We sit in our desks, watching the hands of the clock move towards Saturday night. Tick . . . Tick . . . Tick. King George looks down again from his picture frame. "Hang in there boys," he whispers to us. "It's already Wednesday." We wait forever, and then suddenly, it's Hockey Night in Canada, and we're flopping down on the chesterfield at home, to listen to Foster Hewitt's play-by-play, live from Maple Leaf Gardens, in faraway Toronto.

Hewitt's voice sounds scratchy on the radio, especially when he gets excited about a breakaway. Sometimes he screeches like the blackboard chalk. All I have to say is that he'd better learn how to pronounce Bucyk. He's going to shout it at the top of his lungs plenty of times in his life.

I guess I'll have to learn to skate first. The trouble is I'm already ten years old and I don't have any skates.

This has been a hard year for me. My Dad died, and my Mum has to work extra hard to buy the groceries for our family. "Sorry, Johnny, there's no money left over for new hockey skates," she said. She didn't have to tell me. I already knew.

"I'll give you my old skates as soon as I outgrow them," my brother Bill told me when she'd left the kitchen table. "I'll make you a rink in the backyard, too."

When we play hockey for money Bill and I are going to buy Mum everything she needs.

They say to be a good hockey player, you have to come from Canada. Too bad there isn't an NHL team in our hometown, eh? Can you imagine an NHL team captain carrying the Stanley Cup above his shoulders in front of a cheering crowd in Edmonton? It will never happen in a million years. This town is just too small.

I'll have to move away from the West to play professional hockey. I'll probably end up in Toronto or Montreal, or Detroit or Boston. Wherever I go in my life, I'll remember that the most exciting game in the world is played in one corner of hockey heaven. North Edmonton.

The Chocolate Bar War

Three cents isn't a lot of money. Maybe you think we're crazy to make such a fuss over three pathetic pennies.

How can we explain it? We love our chocolate bars.

The trouble started on April 25, 1947—a rotten day in Canadian history if ever there was one—when the price of a chocolate bar rose from five cents to eight cents.

Did those candy millionaires think we were made of dollar bills? We had paid a nickel for a chocolate bar for our entire lives.

All over Canada kids started to grumble. On Vancouver Island some students made signs and stood outside a candy shop to protest the bad news. Five days later, two hundred kids ran through the doors of the British Columbia legislature in Victoria. "Bring back our nickel bars!" they shouted.

A newspaper reporter wrote a story about it, and soon we were listening to reports about the chocolate bar war on CJCA here in Edmonton. The radio said high-school students in Toronto organized a big protest, and little kids in New Brunswick made homemade fudge from their sugar rations to show those chocolate companies who was boss.

We decided to do something right here in Edmonton. From Beverly to West Jasper Place, from Garneau up to Calder, we made homemade signs and armbands, and we rode our bikes to

the candy stores. "Don't be a sucker!" we yelled to the other kids. "Don't buy eight-cent bars!"

This is probably the first time in Edmonton's history that kids have gone on strike.

Don't be shocked. We're still going to school. We still spend our nickels and dimes on Edmonton's most delicious treats. We buy Charlie Hepburn's potato chips at his potato chip factory on 124th Street, and Sam Cherniak's mouth-watering popcorn at his cart downtown. We're not cheapskates. We buy Batman and Superman comic books at Bill's Book Exchange on 97th Street. We buy movie tickets to see Rin Tin Tin at the Roxy. We buy model airplanes at the Happy Hobbies store on 100th Street.

We just won't buy another chocolate bar until the price comes down. Not a chance.

Our chocolate bar strike isn't easy. We walk past the corner store on a Friday afternoon, with our stomachs rumbling, trying not to look through the window. One day we saw a police officer on Whyte Avenue unwrapping a bar of delicious milk chocolate—with almonds—very slowly, right in front of our noses. "Want some, kids?" he said with a laugh. Very funny, sergeant.

If only we could go on strike against kidney beans or turnips or Cod liver oil. Why doesn't the price ever go up on spinach?

We won't end our chocolate bar war until we teach those candy manufacturers a lesson. Eight cents is robbery! We're not buying!

How much do you pay for a chocolate bar?

The Night of the Orange Sky

When I was little, I had to have an afternoon nap every day. One day when I was five years old my mother made me stay in bed for an extra-long time.

"Why can't I get up now, Momma?" I asked.

"We're going for a car ride after dark tonight," she said. "We want you to be awake."

We never left home after dark, so I was curious.

"Where are we going?"

"Daddy is taking us to the edge of Edmonton to see something that can only be seen at night." she said. "City people can't see it because the streetlights are too bright. It's something special we'll enjoy."

It was hard to stay in bed. I kept trying to think of what this special thing could be. I listened to quiet voices coming from the next room. I heard my father say: "We should wake her now."

I got dressed quickly. Daddy helped me with my coat. Our car was parked at the curb and my mother helped me into the back seat. She tucked me under the red plaid car blanket and handed me a package wrapped in waxed paper. "Here's a sandwich in case you're hungry." She sat in the front seat beside my father.

As we drove down 76th Avenue I looked out the back window. Our house got smaller and smaller. Then I couldn't see it at all.

We hadn't lived in our house for long. We had moved a lot. Three months before I was born, my father, who was in the Royal Canadian Air Force, went away to the war. My mother and I lived with my grandmother in her big, brick house in Strathcona until he came back. My mother said it was hard to find a place to live right after the war. We lived in my other grandparents' house for a year. There were so few places to live in Edmonton that the government built hundreds of houses, and the men who had been in the war had the first chance at claiming one. That's how we were lucky enough to get our little house in Ritchie.

As I looked out the window the car turned in a new direction, not towards my grandparents' houses, or my cousins' house on the north side of the river, but the opposite way. We were in a place I didn't know.

We drove on a bumpy road past the last house and streetlights at the edge of the city. I saw nothing but trees, bushes and tall grass for a long time. My nose tickled with dust. I wasn't sure I liked being here. I slid down on the seat so I couldn't see the bushes rushing by.

The car turned again and suddenly the sky was wasn't black anymore. It was a soft yellow blur that changed colour as we watched.

"Look at that!" my mother said in an amazed voice. It looked like the sky was on fire.

Dad stopped the car. We stood in an empty field, looking up. Dad helped us climb to the roof of the car so we could see better. The light bounced back and forth between the low clouds, changing from yellow to orange to red. I pointed to places where the ground met the sky. It looked like giant candles were shooting flames into the clouds.

"Those are flares," my father said. He said men put big pipes into the ground to get at something called oil. The holes were called wells.

"Why are they burning up the ground?" I asked.

"It looks that way, but they are really burning the part they can't use," he explained. "They set it on fire to get rid of it."

He said the oil could be made into other things like gas to make cars go, and someday it would heat houses all over Canada. I thought about that. The winter before, my blanket had frozen to the wall of my room because our house was so cold. In the rush to get the new houses ready some things were left out. Although it was winter, and very cold, my dad had to crawl under the house and into the attic to add a thick layer of insulation to keep the wind out.

My Dad squeezed my hand. His hand was warm.

"There's probably enough oil in the ground, Karen, to keep every house in Canada warm in the coldest winter—even our house," he said. "This is going to make big changes in our world."

I looked at the sky, and tried to imagine what he meant.

Why July is Perfect

Do you love July as much as I do? I think you do.

You wake up on the first morning and say to yourself: "No school! I'm free all day!" The shivers of an Edmonton winter are packed up in a cardboard box with the mitts, scarves, and woolly hats. The sun is high and hot.

Your July begins in a red-and-white T-shirt on Canada Day, with bike parades, a picnic at Hawrelak Park, and booming fireworks over the North Saskatchewan River. After that comes Klondike Days with the giant parade through downtown streets, the raft races on the river, and the scary but exciting rides at K-Days.

My July is different, but it's perfect, too.

I wade into the cool, blue water of Waką mne. In the language of the Nakoda people, my people, Waką mne means God's Lake. The Cree name for our lake is Manito Sâkâhikan. The English and French name is Lac Ste. Anne. Maybe you've seen this beautiful lake, because it's close to Edmonton and St. Albert.

I've lived near the lake all my life at my home on the Alexis reserve, although I go to Edmonton on the bus to shop sometimes. Once I went to the Camsell Hospital to get my tonsils out, and another time when I cut my knee.

I spoke only the Stoney language until I went to kindergarten. Do you know the old Nakoda name for Edmonton? It was *Ti Oda*, which means Many Houses. Would you like to learn some summer words? Say: *Moso macashdahwan*. That means: "I might go swimming."

Every July—for five perfect days—tens of thousands of people travel to my community to visit the healing waters of Lac Ste. Anne. They come from all over Edmonton, and all over Alberta. They come from Saskatchewan, British Columbia, and Manitoba, even as far away as the Northwest Territiories and Montana. Year after year, they keep coming back.

I call this time *Aba Tã* which means a very special time. To me it's like Christmas in July.

"Are you awake yet, Kathleen?"

That's probably my grandfather at the front door. He is joking with me, of course, because he knows I wake up early on the first morning of the pilgrimage. He brings apples, oranges, and Fig Newton cookies to my brothers and sisters and me when he visits our house. We love the treats he keeps in his pockets for us, and we love him.

My grandfather knows we wait for this day all year. In the middle of July we begin to watch out for the first weary people as they walk up the dusty road in their bare feet. My grandfather says these visitors pray as they walk for miles from Edmonton to our lake. "It's one of the traditions," he says, "but there are many more."

People have been coming here every summer for a hundred years, maybe a thousand years, he says. Some pray in the traditional way. Some pray in the Christian way. Some pray both ways. Elders believe the water of Wakã mne has the power to heal the sick, and make sad people feel much better. Old people say they have beautiful dreams here. When elders hear drumming on the rock island, they know the spirits of their ancestors are not far away. For them this will always be a sacred place.

"You have to behave very well this week," my grandfather says. "I'll be watching to see that you do."

Munching an apple I ask him how he will find me in such a huge crowd of people.

"I'll be there," he said. "And all of your relatives will watching out for you, too."

That's a lot of people! Can you imagine how excited you'd be if thousands of strangers—and hundreds of relatives you'd never met—arrived in your neighbourhood every July to camp in the park near your house? My friends and I play tag between tents and tipis, pick-up trucks and camper trailers. We explore every corner of the campsite; watch the little kids playing tag; smell the hamburgers cooking over the campfires; touch the turquoise rings and necklaces for sale on the long tables; spy on the teenagers as they listen to the Beatles on their transistor radios.

Everyone seems to be smiling. It feels good to live in a place that makes other people so happy.

In the afternoon I'll wade into the lake with my family. We'll fill jugs full of water to bless our house, and to use as medicine through the year. Some people will go into the lake on crutches;

some elders and sick people will be carried into the healing water to pray.

One evening this week, when the sun goes down, I'll walk with hundreds of people in a long procession beside the lake. We'll hold candles in our hands. Our candlelight will make the lake shimmer in the darkness. In the distance we'll see the orange glow of a hundred campfires, and hear echoes of laughter across the water. This is a place of stories and prayers, sweetgrass and woodsmoke. This is my perfect July.

When I was smaller, I remember riding on a wagon with other Alexis kids as we made our way to the lake. When the wagon crossed the bridge I looked down, terrified, because I was sure we would tumble into the water. Now I'm nine, and the bridge doesn't look scary anymore. The water doesn't seem as deep.

Some summer when I'm older I'll walk on the dusty road in my bare feet with the other people. I'll pray to St. Anne that the pilgrimage to Wakã mne will happen every July for the rest of my life, and a thousand years after that, for all the kids who come this way.

James's Discovery

You'll never guess what I found near Whitemud Creek.

Almost every weekend I explore the river valley with my older brother Michael and my mum. We live in a townhouse in Michener Park, but we come down here on Saturday mornings to look for fossils and stuff. Last Saturday was my lucky day. We were exploring along the creek in Rainbow Valley. First, my mum found some petrified wood in the dirt under a pipeline. When she dusted it off, it looked like large teeth, about six centimetres long.

"They could be dinosaur teeth!" she said, all excited. We started to search the ground like detectives, pulling away rocks with our hands, and looking through the dirt for prehistoric clues.

I walked behind Michael and Mum to a searching place of my own under the same pipeline. I found this blue-coloured fossil, and I liked the shape of it.

"Just fungus," Mum said, "but let's keep it."

She was so thrilled about the dinosaur teeth she'd found. After lunch she wrapped our discoveries in a dish towel, and put them in a cardboard box. We rode the bus to the Provincial Museum of Alberta, carrying the box as if it were a pirate's chest full of diamonds and gold. The bus driver gave us a weird look.

We went to see Jim Burns. He's the palaeontologist, the fossil expert at the museum. He opened the box and carefully unwrapped the dish towel.

"Yes, they're teeth—horses' teeth, perhaps six hundred years old," he told my mother. Dinosaurs did live in Edmonton's river valley long ago, but I guess they refused to leave their teeth behind for my mother's satisfaction. She looked a bit disappointed.

A minute later Jim picked up the blue fungus I'd found. "I'm more interested in this," he said. He stopped talking for a moment. You could tell he was excited because his hands shook a little bit.

"I have a hunch I know what this is," he said. "But before I can say for sure, it will have to go through many scientific tests."

A few weeks later Jim called our house with the amazing news.

"This is the milk tooth of a mastodon, a giant prehistoric animal that lived in our river valley long, long before human beings," he said. "This rare tooth is somewhere between twenty-two thousand and forty thousand years old."

I can't believe I found it. I'm eight years old. Why me?

Jim says they will keep the mastodon tooth in the museum collection because it is so rare. That's probably a good idea. Do you think I should have hidden the tooth under a rock, somewhere along Whitemud Creek, so another Edmonton kid could discover it in the year 4004? Too bad I didn't think of that. Maybe next time!

Angela and the Tornado

Yesterday when the sky over Edmonton turned purple and black I discovered I was brave.

My name is Angela. I was in the Evergreen Mobile Home Park when a tornado twisted its way along the edge of Edmonton, over the river, and up to our neighbourhood in the city's top corner. The tornado wrecked everything it touched.

Tonight I'm sleeping on a couch in a stranger's house.

I know what you're thinking. You probably want to tell me that I'm lucky to be safe, that I'll find a new home soon. I can almost hear you saying to me: "Everyone in this city loves you. Now go to sleep."

How can I go to sleep? I stare at the ceiling, and think about every single thing that happened yesterday.

I remember the scrambled eggs and toast I ate for breakfast. I remember the hot, sticky weather in the afternoon. I remember riding my bike, and eating popsicles, when the thunderstorm began.

"Better get inside," said my mum, looking at the sky.

Have you ever heard the wind howling and shrieking for no good reason? Chico Bulmer banged on neighbours' doors, and yelled, "Follow me. Don't be scared. Run for the basement of the hall!"

We didn't hear him. We saw the black whirlwind through the window. "Lie down flat!" my mother shouted, pushing us down behind the couch. I crouched with my brother Greg and cousin Jamie and my two-year-old brother Michael. We didn't have time to cry.

We heard a huge roar, and the smashing, crashing of our windows. Everything shook. I thought the sky was tumbling down on our heads.

Suddenly the roar stopped.

We heard crying and yelling, then sirens. Then we heard the most beautiful sound I've ever heard, a man's voice. "I'm here," he shouted. "Can I help you? Call out to me!" I pulled myself to a hole where a window used to be. I saw the stranger, and waved my hand out to him. "Help us!" I yelled.

"I'll be right there," he replied. "Keep calm. Everything will be alright."

He helped my mum and the rest of my family into his truck. He drove as fast as he could to Alberta Hospital. I think we were the first family in the door. Doctors and nurses came running to meet us. I didn't know that we'd been injured until I saw myself in the mirror in the hospital bathroom. Later the stranger drove us to his trailer because we didn't have a home anymore.

Edmonton will never get another storm like that one, my Mum says, but I can't stop looking at the sky.

Don't worry about tornadoes. Just remember that if a day ever comes when you need to be brave, you will be. Just like the kids at Evergreen.

Hockey English

One thing you can say about me is that I'm a world traveller. My family moved from northern Iraq, to Iran, back to Iraq, and to Turkey, looking for a safe place to live. We came to Edmonton in 1998 to start over again.

Our suitcases got lost on the way to Canada so we had nothing at all from home when we arrived at the International Airport. That didn't feel too good. The man at the Immigration desk gave me a warm jacket, some winter boots, and wool mitts for my hands. He said something to me about Canada—maybe about the winter here, maybe about hockey—but I just shook my head back and forth.

I was six years old at the time. English was a secret code, and I didn't know it yet.

A woman named Kelly came to meet us at the airport. "Hello, Jwamer," she said, kneeling down to talk to me. She smiled and talked to us in slow, quiet English, and then she hugged my parents, my sisters Niga and Ewar, and me. She had a kind voice, but I didn't understand her either. Not a word.

Edmonton looked very strange to me at first. Kelly drove us in her car down a long highway, past many stores and high buildings, to the top of a hill. We stared at the twinkling lights on the other side of a twisting river. In the valley I saw four pyramids,

like in Egypt, only smaller and made of glass, and I wondered what they could be.

We drove down the hill, over the river on a rumbling, humming bridge, and up the hill on the other side. We needed an hour just to drive across the city to the Reception Centre. I was so tired I fell asleep right away.

Our first home in Edmonton was a townhouse in Castledowns. People in our neighbourhood come from all over the world. I spoke Kurdish with my parents and sisters at home, until the day I started school. I remember how scared I was when I walked into the playground. I tried hard to remember the few English words in my head, but they were all jumbled up with Kurdish and Turkish words.

I learned to speak English in six months. No kidding. My teacher was amazed. My new friends were amazed. My parents were even more amazed. The teacher explained to them that I was learning faster than the rest of my family because I'm the youngest, and kids have more room in their brains for new languages.

To tell you the truth there was another reason.

I had invented a special method of learning English when nobody was watching.

Every Saturday night I settled down on the couch and clicked on the TV to watch Hockey Night in Canada. I was born in a country where everybody played soccer—we called it *topane* in Kurdish—but I learned to love this fast game on ice. I watched every game on TV in that cold first winter.

I remember my favourite words in English after that: Oilers, hockey, ice, skates, Northlands, NHL, Oilers, goalie, puck, Doug Weight, Oilers, Bill Ranford, Oilers, Coliseum, rink, face-off, defenceman, Oilers, blue line, power play, forward, Oilers, offside, body check, penalty, sudden death overtime, he shoots, he scores!

Did I say Oilers? Did I say hockey? I was learning how to speak English with an Edmonton accent. I was starting to feel at home.

Bradley's Whirlwind
Tour of Edmonton

I've lived in Edmonton since the day I was born so I know the city pretty well.

If new kids came here from the other side of the world—from Vietnam, or India, or Nigeria, or Russia—I'd be happy to give them a tour of my favourite places.

Don't worry. I wouldn't take them on one of those ordinary bus tours. I wouldn't say: "On your right, you will see this boring building. On your left, you will see that boring building."

No way. Forget buildings. Forget the bus.

I would hire the world's fastest racecar driver to drive us around the city in the world's fastest race car. I love fast cars. We'd zoom up Wayne Gretzky Drive, out the Yellowhead, down the Anthony Henday, along the Whitemud, down the Calgary Trail, up Gateway Boulevard, along the Fort Road, and out Manning Freeway. The visiting kids would be dizzy with all the curves on the Groat Road. We'd cross the High Level Bridge twice just for the heck of it.

I guess we would have to obey the speed limit or a police officer would stop us. Once somebody asked me: "Is there anything in Edmonton you think needs improvement?" I said the police in this city give out too many speeding tickets.

On the tour I would ask the racecar driver to slow down a bit in front of the Royal Alexandra Hospital. That's where I was born.

"On to West Edmonton Mall!" I'd shout from the back seat.

My favourite place in the entire city is the Playdium at West Ed. My favourite spot in the Playdium is right in front of the DDR game. DDR stands for Dance Dance Revolution. You stand on this floor panel, and watch pink and blue arrows flash on the video screen. The trick is to move your feet very quickly to touch the matching arrows on the floor panel as the techno music speeds up, faster and faster, and the arrows keep moving. I love it!

It won't surprise you that my other favourite game at Playdium is Initial D, a racecar video game. You choose a video character and a video car, and you zoom toward the video horizon with no speed limit and no speeding tickets.

After we'd finished playing video games at the Playdium, I'd take my new friends on a two-hour tour of Canada's largest shopping mall. Their eyes would be wide with amazement, but their feet would be really sore. We'd cool off with a swim through the waves at the water park, Edmonton's indoor ocean, and then we'd relax on the indoor beach.

The racecar driver would wait patiently outside West Ed, revving his engine, until we were ready to go.

"Could you take us back to my place, please?" I'd ask.

He'd turn the key in the ignition, and we'd zoom north to 158th Avenue. Almost by magic, five new bikes and bike helmets would appear at the curb for the visitors and me.

"Come on!" I'd say. "Let's go!"

I'd lead them on a speedy bike ride through my neighbourhood, and over to the playground. We'd play basketball and soccer until we were exhausted, and then we'd go back to my place to watch sports on TV and eat something good.

Maybe the girl from Nigeria would ask me what other kids liked to do in Edmonton for fun.

In summer, I'd explain, some kids like to ride on the paddleboats at Hawrelak Park, and bump into each other. Some go wading in their soaking-wet clothes in the pools outside City Hall and the Alberta Legislature. Others go skateboarding at Sir Winston Churchill Square, or rollerblading at Terwilligar Park. Some ride their bikes along the bike trails as far as they go, following the river. Others go with their families to Fort Edmonton Park or the Ukrainian Heritage Village to explore outdoor museums about the past. Some kids like to stare into the big, brown eyes of the buffalo in paddocks at Elk Island National Park.

Maybe the boy from China would ask what Edmonton's kids do in the winter.

Some build snow forts for snowball fights, I'd say. Others play this game where you walk along the top of a snowbank and see how many steps you can take before your winter boots fall through the snow crust. Some kids skate a lot—hockey, figure skating, and wobbly skating—in arenas and shopping malls, on large outdoor rinks and small backyard rinks. Kids go tobogganing or snowboarding on Canada's best sliding hills, like the high hill at Rundle Park.

On winter Saturdays, when it's really cold, they go to movies at the dollar theatres, or they rent computer games for sleepovers. They play indoor hockey and indoor soccer, and they take swimming lessons in indoor swimming pools.

"I prefer basketball myself," I'd say.

If the kid from Vietnam asked me what I liked best about Edmonton, I would be able to answer in English or in Vietnamese: *Đây là một thành phố rất tốt và đồng bào ở đây cũng rất tốt.* That means, "It's a nice place with nice people." It's where I live. It's home.

Welcome to our Birthday Party

For thousands of years kids have made a home in this river valley. Today we're celebrating Edmonton's 100th year as a city.

Happy birthday, Edmonton, from all of us.

What Happened Next?

The Edmonton stories you've read in this book are based on real kids, and their true experiences. Here's what we know—and what we don't know—about each one.

The First Ones: Nobody knows when human beings first visited the place where Edmonton exists today. Archaeologists find many clues like stone tools and ancient fire pits when they dig for evidence in the North Saskatchewan River valley. They believe kids have camped around here with their families for at least 8,000 years, maybe longer.

We Walked Across the Prairies: Unfortunately, we will never know the names of the children who travelled with Anthony Henday and his companions Attickasish and Connawapa in 1755. Henday, a traveller and trader with the Hudson's Bay Company, wrote an interesting diary about his important trip to what is now Alberta. "We are twelve in number: nine women and children," he wrote when he was here, but he didn't identify the family members.

When he wrote about his important visit with the Archithinue people, he was talking about the people we know today as the Blackfoot, or Siksika, or *nitsitapii*.

Some historians believe Henday and his friends walked along the frozen river through our river valley, below what is now downtown Edmonton, and camped near the place where Fort Saskatchewan stands today. They say some of the kids with him might have been his own Métis children. Other historians say Henday's diary is unreliable about the location of their campsites, and their travel route.

Jimmy Jock: Jimmy Jock Bird became an apprentice to the Hudson's Bay

Company at the age of 11, and a clerk at 18. In those days it was common for children to work for their living.

Born at Edmonton House in 1800, Jimmy Jock was the son of James Curtis Bird, an English-speaking fur trader, and a Cree woman, Oomenahowish, who was known to her husband as Mary. When Jimmy Jock was a boy, the Hudson's Bay Company post was usually called Edmonton House. The North West Company post, Fort Augustus, was nearby. Have you ever watched a baseball game at Telus Field? That's near the location of the two forts when Jimmy Jock was a kid. Visitors like Marie-Anne Gaboury Lagimodière often commented on the riding skill of the Métis and First Nations children who lived in this area.

Jimmy Jock was an adventurer and a traveller all his life. When he was a young man, Chief Factor John Rowand, the man called Iron Shirt, sent him to trade among the First Nations of the southern plains. Jimmy Jock married Sally Peigan, daughter of Bull's Heart, around 1825 at Belly River. They had eleven children, and travelled all over the West together for over sixty-five years.

Jimmy Jock paid his last visit to Edmonton, to tell stories to his nephew William Bird, in 1890. He died at Two Medicine Creek, Montana in 1892. Many descendants of the Bird family live in Edmonton today.

The Hidden Boys: Two boys did leave Fort Edmonton hidden in saddlebags. We know about them because Sir George Simpson, a Hudson's Bay Company boss, wrote their story down in 1841. He described how they arrived at the trading post, and how everyone searched for them when they disappeared. Unfortunately he did not record their names.

By that time the Hudson's Bay Company trading post had moved to a place just below where the Alberta Legislature stands today. The name had changed from Edmonton House to Fort Edmonton over the years. Fort Augustus didn't exist anymore.

Simpson suggested the boys were kidnapped, but Alberta historian Hugh Dempsey says it is more likely their relatives came to bring them home to their families on the plains.

Victoria's Promise: As she promised in the story, Victoria Belcourt Callihoo did live to be 105.

She was born in 1861, at a time when Queen Victoria ruled the British Empire from her throne in England. Victoria grew up in a well-known Métis family with deep roots in the Edmonton area. She was the daughter of buffalo hunter and guide Alexis Belcourt and medicine woman Nancy Rowand. Victoria was a great-granddaughter of John Rowand, who was the chief factor, or boss, at Fort Edmonton for many years.

When Victoria grew up she married Louis Jerome Callihoo. The couple raised their thirteen children around Lac Ste. Anne. Victoria was known all her life for her ability as a traditional healer. She had an excellent memory, too. In her old age she gave many interviews about Métis traditions of this area, and the last buffalo hunts before the herds disappeared and a western way of life ended. She danced at her 100th birthday party in St. Albert. She died in 1966.

Annie Laurie's Moose Ride: Annie Laurie Robertson arrived at Fort Edmonton in 1883 at the age of seven, after an exciting trip across the

Prairies. She travelled by train with her family to the end of the railway tracks at Fort Calgary, where her father was waiting with a horse and wagon to take them north. The Robertsons lived in a tent on the riverbank at first, then moved into a homemade log house on the spot where the Hotel Macdonald now stands. At that time only a few hundred people lived in the settlement.

From the beginning Annie Laurie loved to play hockey. As a teenager she was the captain of the Edmonton girls' hockey team. She is the player on the far left in this photo. Her father was the sheriff, something like a police officer. "Though I had a very unusual childhood, I had a very happy one," she said later in her life. "We had horses to ride, that is Indian ponies, which we kept in a corral next to the house on the hill. It is hard to believe, looking at the beautiful Hotel Macdonald, that at one time a haystack decked the riverbank, rabbits frolicking about. My brother Fred and I have many times snared rabbits on what is now Jasper Avenue." She wrote the true story about the moose ride for her grandchildren before her death in 1964.

Billy's Trick: Billy Griesbach was eight when the Northwest Rebellion began in 1885. He told this story about his cat in a book he wrote about his life called *I Remember*.

New settlers in Edmonton, St. Albert, and the Fort Saskatchewan district were nervous during the Rebellion. They believed many rumours about the threats to their safety, and they hid at Fort Edmonton and in St. Albert churches.

In the end, no fighting happened in this area, and nobody was hurt. Arthur Griesbach, Billy's father, led the North West Mounted Police at their base at Fort Saskatchewan. We know the police force today as the RCMP, or the Mounties for short.

Bobtail was a very important Cree chief. He has many descendants who live in Hobbema and Edmonton. The chiefs in the Edmonton area, Papastayo, Michel Callihoo, Alexander, Alexis and Enoch all decided to stay out of the Rebellion, but they told the Canadian government to keep the promises it made in Treaty 6.

Lawrence Garneau, also mentioned in the story, was a Métis settler in south Edmonton who was falsely accused of treason during the Rebellion, and jailed for a short time. The Garneau neighbourhood near the University of Alberta is named after his big family.

Billy grew up to be known as William Griesbach. As a teenager he won prizes as a cyclist, soccer player and hockey player. Later he became a city councillor, the mayor of Edmonton and a Member of Parliament for Edmonton. As a commanding officer in the First World War, he recruited one thousand Alberta men and led them into battle.

Returning to Edmonton, he finally lived with his family in a big, brick house on Stony Plain Road.

Eliza's Treaty: Eliza Papastew Gladu was born in 1880, the daughter of Chief Papastayo and one of his wives, Lucie. Altogether Eliza had fifteen brothers and sisters. The chief, whose Cree family name is also spelled Papaschase, Passpasschase, or Papastew in English, brought his band into Treaty 6 in 1877. The treaty promised land to every family. The government of Canada laid out a reserve for 241 band members on the south

shore of the river in 1880. At first the Papaschase reserve covered forty-eight square miles, between the North Saskatchewan River and Ellerslie. Later the Government of Canada offered some people in the Papaschase band some money, took back the land, and sold it to Edmonton's new settlers.

The last Papaschase members left the reserve on orders from the government on August 11, 1877, although many had left earlier. Some families moved to the Enoch reserve at Stony Plain, but others moved all across the West.

Eliza grew up and married Tchanepiw, also known as Joseph Paul. She raised her children on the Kehewin reserve, but her family did eventually come back to her birthplace. Her great-great-great grandchildren live in Edmonton today.

Our Raft Trip to A New Home: Maria Yureichuk, the mother of the children on the raft, told the story of their challenging trip from Edmonton to their first homestead when she was an older woman.

Thousands of Ukrainian settlers came to the territory we now call Alberta after 1893. Back then they were known as Galicians or Bukhovinians. The Canadian government offered free land to settlers who would agree to plough and plant crops, and build a home. The Ukrainians had a long and difficult journey to the West. Thousands settled on homesteads north and east of

Edmonton. Many early Ukrainian pioneers worked in coal mines in Beverly; in the railway yards in Calder; and in many other city jobs, too. Thousands of their descendants live in Edmonton today, and they continue to honour Ukrainian traditions.

The Day the Edmonton Police Banned Tobogganing: Edgar Nobles told this tobogganing story to researchers who tucked it away in a file at the City of Edmonton Archives, the place where the city keeps its treasured stories and photographs. You can visit the Archives at the Prince of Wales Armouries, just beside Victoria School for the Performing Arts. The building looks like a big castle.

Edgar moved here with his family in 1906, two years after the town of 18,500 people began to call itself a city. He remembers that Edmonton had only two paved sidewalks at the time. Kids loved tobogganing then as much as they do now, but they usually called it sledding or coasting.

The arrival of four streetcars in 1908 changed their sledding habits on downtown hills. A streetcar was like a small train that ran on tracks down the streets and avenues before buses, something like the LRT. The last streetcar stopped running in 1951. In 2004 Edmonton had almost eight hundred buses and thirty-seven LRT trains.

Edgar said his favourite summer pastime in the summer was a ride to Big Island on a riverboat called The Edmonton. "We used to get on at the wharf next to John Walter's mill," he said. The trip would take four or five hours, with an orchestra playing on deck, and a picnic on the island. You can still take a riverboat ride on the Edmonton Queen, but it doesn't go as far as Big Island because the river is too shallow now.

High Level Hijinks: Grace lived in Strathcona with her brothers and sisters and parents when the south part of Edmonton was a separate town. Later the two towns joined together to become a city. Grace's father, David Duggan, was elected the Mayor of Edmonton. He was the first person to

broadcast words over the radio in the city. Grace said her father was very surprised to find out that his words could be heard all the way to his house on the south side of the river! She told stories about her childhood in an interview for the City of Edmonton Archives.

The High Level Bridge was built in 1913, and it is still Edmonton's highest bridge.

Fred's Flood: Fred Barnes told this story about the flood to interviewers from the City of Edmonton Archives in 1970.

The emergency began on Sunday, June 27, 1915. Thousands of people watched from the high riverbanks as the North Saskatchewan rose fourteen metres and spilled across the small neighbourhoods on the flats: Riverdale, Rossdale, and Cloverdale were covered with water. Large houses, stables, and shacks crashed into the bridges. To save the Low Level Bridge city workers loaded sand on a string of freight train cars, then sent the train on the bridge to hold it down. Nearly eight hundred families lost their homes, and many businesses floated away. Hundreds of volunteers rescued stranded people in rowboats and canoes, and cleaned up the big mess.

Most people remember the hard work of washing their muddy houses when the crisis was over. Only one citizen died during the flood. A baby fell from a mother's arms as she waded across a street.

Alfred's Letter: Alfred Bramley-Moore and his family lived a few blocks from the Alberta Legislature when the First World War began in 1914.

Alfred's father, Alwyn Bramley-Moore, was an MLA in the Legislature who wrote a book about Alberta's future.

When the First World War began, Alfred's father left Edmonton to

become a soldier. He wrote many letters to his children Alfred, Laura, Dorothy, William, and Gladys, before his death in the battlefield in France in April, 1916.

You can find the family letters and photographs in an interesting book called *The Path of Duty* by Ken Tingley.

As a grownup Alfred took his father's advice to "stick to Alberta." He became a lawyer in Edmonton, and died here in 1981. His little sister Gladys recently celebrated her ninety-fifth birthday. She still remembers every detail of the day her family heard the news about her father's death, and her long walk home from school.

The First World War lasted from 1914 to 1918. Hundreds of Edmonton men and women joined the military, and many men died in the fighting.

Gertrude's Castle: Gertrude Dahl grew up to be a teacher at Bellevue School. She and her husband raised their children in the Highlands neighbourhood.

When Gertrude's grandchildren were small they would ask her about the china plates on her wall. Each one had a picture of a different building in Edmonton, and a story to match. Gertrude loved to tell them about visiting her father when he baked treats at the beautiful castle on the hill.

Sometime in the 1920s Rudolph Jacob took his recipes from the Hotel Macdonald down the street to a very popular restaurant that became known as American Dairy Lunch. This café was owned by the Spillios family, who had come from Greece. The restaurant doesn't exist anymore, but older people still remember the delicious food and the happy atmosphere of the place.

Fortunately the Hotel Macdonald still stands proudly at the corner of Jasper Avenue and 100th Street. The castle hotel was named after Canada's first prime minister, Sir John A. Macdonald. If you peek from the front lobby into the bar, you will see a huge painting of Sir John A. and the Fathers of Confederation on the wall.

The hotel stood empty for many years, but it reopened in 1991 after a beautiful renovation. Some people say a ghost haunts the hallways. The hotel's new name is the Fairmont Macdonald, but like everyone in Edmonton, Gertrude still calls it "The Mac."

Peace in Flight: Peace Cornwall Hudson grew up to travel all over the globe, but she said her favourite place in the world was the Groat Ravine. She and her sister, Norah, told interesting stories about Edmonton in the 1920s to interviewers at the City of Edmonton Archives.

The daring pilot in the story, Wop May, grew up in Edmonton, too. His real name was Wilfrid, but he got his nickname from a little cousin who called him "Wop" because she couldn't pronounce his name.

Wop May became famous for his bravery as a pilot in the First World War. Later he was one of Edmonton's most famous northern bush pilots. He showed great courage in delivering medicine to Alberta's north country during an epidemic, flying in an open plane in winter with his co-pilot Vic Horner. He was also a great stunt flyer, and he really did fly under the High Level Bridge to drop a baseball to a pitcher at a game on Rossdale Flats. If you'd like to know more about the adventures of Edmonton's famous pilot Wop May, read *Wings of a Hero* by Sheila Reid.

Odilé's New Shoes: Odilé David Samwald grew up in Edmonton during the hard times of the 1930s, the Depression. It was very difficult for adults to find jobs then. Grownups who did find jobs were not paid very much. Sometimes kids quit school at a young age to help their families earn money.

Many families relied on relief—small payments that would give them enough money for food and rent, but not much else. When Odilé was nine—a year after this story took place—she contracted polio, a disease that Edmonton's children don't get anymore. That's why she is in a wheelchair in this picture.

One day, when Odilé had grown up, she met Miss Hanley again. She tried to thank her for the Christmas present, but by then her teacher was too old and frail to understand what she was saying. Like Miss Hanley, Odilé gave many years of her life to Edmonton's students. She grew up to become a teacher at Archbishop O'Leary High School. Now retired in St. Albert, she would like to dedicate her story to her granddaughter, Radhika Samwald.

Peter's War: Peter was the only Jewish refugee child admitted to Canada alone by a special order of the prime minister and his cabinet before the Second World War.

Harry and Frances Friedman worked hard for a year to bring Peter

to Edmonton from Frankfurt, Germany. After many letters, rejections and appeals, they succeeded in 1938.

Peter was a student at Westglen High School during the Second World War. Later he studied at the University of Alberta, and became a lawyer. When he was old enough, and the war in Europe was over, he brought his parents to live in Edmonton with more help from the Friedmans. He served the community as the leader of the University of Alberta Hospital Board, and president of the Edmonton Art Gallery, among many other volunteer activities. Today he lives in the Oliver neighbourhood.

Attention! It's Time to Mention Our Inventions!: Bob Davies has created an amazing homemade book about Edmonton when he was your

age: including his sketches and photographs of toys, games, parades, parks and playgrounds and kids' favourite city places. He has also written about his days in the Edmonton Schoolboys' Band, a famous marching band that attracted kids from all over the city for many years, and many other stories about his adventures.

When Bob grew up he worked for the city in the Water Department, and he got to know every street and avenue very well. He lives in Victoria, BC which we sometimes call Edmonton West because many city people go there when they retire.

So far Bob's book has not been published, but you can find a copy of it in the City of Edmonton Archives.

Hockey Hero of 65th Street: John Bucyk inherited his brother Bill's second-hand skates before his eleventh birthday. He said he wasn't a good skater at first, but he kept practising. He shovelled the snow off hockey rinks in the days before zambonis to get free ice time. His brother Bill also became an excellent hockey player. John starred with the Edmonton Oil Kings and the Edmonton Flyers before he began to play for the Detroit Red Wings and Boston Bruins. He earned $6,500 for the entire season in his first contract with Detroit, but the team also found him a job. He loved working with cars, and continued working as a mechanic for thirteen years while he was playing with the NHL.

John played 21 seasons as a Bruin, scored 545 goals, and broke many team records. His team won the Stanley Cup in 1970 and 1972, and after a long and successful career, he was inducted into the Hockey Hall of Fame in 1981.

The Edmonton Mercurys brought home an Olympic gold medal from Oslo, Norway in 1952, but hockey-loving Edmonton waited a long time for its own NHL team. The Edmonton Oilers won five NHL championships in the 1980s; their captain, Wayne Gretzky, often held up the Stanley Cup over his shoulders as the city cheered on its hockey heroes.

In his book about his life, *Hockey Is In My Blood,* John Bucyk said his favourite Christmas gift was his first pair of brand-new skates when he was a teenager. "It sounds funny now, but at that time it was the biggest thrill of my life."

The Chocolate Bar War: Here is a photograph of some Edmonton kids who protested the sudden increase in the price of chocolate bars. On

April 25, 1947, candy companies raised the price from five cents to eight cents. Kids across Canada stopped buying chocolate bars for ten days in protest. Sales fell by 80 per cent.

A newspaper in Toronto, called the *Telegram*, suggested that grown-up Communists fooled Canadian kids into organizing the protest demonstrations across Canada. There was a big scare about Communists at the time. After that the chocolate bar war ended, but many kids remembered their fight for an affordable treat.

The Night of the Orange Sky: Karen Bower remembers the night in 1947 when her parents took her to watch the flares from the Leduc oil

field. The field where they stood is now a busy neighbourhood with many houses.

At 3:55 PM on February 15, 1947, oil gushed from a deep well that became known as Leduc #1. Karen's dad was right. The oil strike did change life for people in Edmonton. Suddenly there were more jobs for grownups, more stores and businesses. Thousands of people began to move to the city from all over Canada and the world. New neighbourhoods, called suburbs, grew up on the edges of the small city, and many families moved from old houses in the centre of Edmonton to new houses in the suburbs. Small towns near Edmonton like Leduc and Devon grew very quickly because of the oil strike, and Sherwood Park appeared a few years later.

The discovery of oil changed Karen's life, too. She moved to Leduc with her parents, Gordon and Grace, in 1949 when her father took a job in the oil service industry. Later she studied history at the University of Washington in Seattle and returned to Edmonton. She held various administrative positions at the University of Alberta before taking early retirement in 2001. She now lives, works, and writes in Vancouver.

Why July is Perfect: Kathleen Alexis grew up on the Alexis reserve near Lac Ste. Anne, just northwest of Edmonton. She was born in 1960, in a big family with eight brothers and sisters. Her grandfather in this story, Joseph Alexis, was the chief of his community for thiry-two years; and one of *his* grandfathers was the Chief Alexis who signed Treaty 6 at a special ceremony near Fort Edmonton in 1877.

"I feel a responsibility to my grandfather to live according to the values he handed down to me," says Kathleen.

The Lac Ste. Anne pilgrimage brings as many as tens of thousands people to the healing waters every summer. The tradition began in 1889 when 171 people came to pray to St. Anne for rain after a long dry spell.

The early French-speaking missionaries named the lake after the grandmother of Jesus, but Lac Ste. Anne has been a sacred place, and a gathering place, for a much longer time. In 1979 archaeologists found the remaining bits of a stone arrowhead or knife here, proving that aboriginal people camped here 5,000 to 6,000 years ago.

Today Kathleen lives in west Edmonton with her family. She works for the Alexis First Nation as a human resources manager, and her husband, Cameron Alexis, has been an RCMP officer for twenty-two years. They have three children, and they still go to the pilgrimage in July.

James's Discovery: James Reininger found the mastodon tooth in 1984 at Rainbow Valley while on a hike with his mother, Catherine, and his brother Michael. He says they always went home from their Saturday hikes with their backpacks full of interesting discoveries, and he is still interested in fossils.

Today James lives in the Mill Woods neighbourhood with his family. He would like to dedicate this story to his new baby, Ameirra Genevieve Cadence Reininger.

Jim Burns still works at the Provincial Museum of Alberta as a palaeontologist. He says the milk tooth of a mastodon is a rare discovery. Only nine have been found in Alberta. A mastodon is a huge prehistoric ancestor of the elephant family.

Angela and the Tornado: Angela Buteau was eight years old when the tornado hit Edmonton's east side on July 31, 1987. Two of her friends died that day.

The tornado killed twenty-seven people, injured hundreds of people, and destroyed many homes and businesses in Edmonton. Among the dead were four citizens under the age of 16: Darcy Reimer, 11; Dawn Reimer, 11; Dianne Reimer, 13 and Sharon Denise Andruchow, 15, all of Evergreen Mobile Home Park.

People in Edmonton worked around the clock to help one another

through the crisis. Volunteers fed homeless families and emergency workers; comforted the injured; donated food, clothing and furniture; and rescued more than one hundred dogs and cats.

To remember the citizens we lost, and the way we helped one another that day, the people of Edmonton built a memorial near the river at Hermitage Park. It shows us with our arms around one another. A graduate of Grant MacEwan College, Angela is continuing her studies at the University of Lethbridge.

Hockey English: Jwamer Barzanji came to Edmonton with his parents and two sisters in 1998 at the age of five. A Kurdish refugee from northern Iraq—the land he calls Kurdistan—he is now a Canadian citizen.

Almost half of the people who live in or around Edmonton today

were born in another place; and about one in six arrived from a different country. Like Jwamer, thousands of kids in the city were born outside Canada.

Now 11, Jwamer goes to school in Castlebrook in suburban north Edmonton, and he still loves hockey. In 2004 he won an award for goaltending for his team, the Avalanche. He says he knows there's only "a one in a million chance" he'll ever be a goalie in the NHL, but why not hope? His other plans are to be a lawyer or an engineer. "I never saw snow or ice until I came to Edmonton," he says. "There was something about gliding on ice that I just loved."

Bradley's Whirlwind Tour of Edmonton: Bradley Pham is ten years old and lives in northwest Edmonton with his family. He likes to play basketball and ride his bike. His parents, Sang and Ha Pham, came to the city in 1980 after a long and difficult journey from Vietnam to Malaysia to Canada. At that time thousands of people were leaving Vietnam, and more than 7,500 came to Alberta to live. Bradley's grandparents and many aunts and uncles came to Canada, too. He has a brother and sister, and his cousin Binh lives in Sherwood Park. When he goes to Vietnam to visit his other relatives, he notices many differences in the food and in the schools. "A lot more people drive motorcycles than cars," he adds.

Bradley doesn't know yet what he wants to do when he grows up, but he knows exactly the kind of car he wants: a fast one, of course. "I'll drive all over the place," he says.

If you'd like to read more true stories about Edmonton's kids: or play interactive games about our city's history—visit the Web site: www.kidmonton.ca

Photo credits:

Jimmy Jock Bird: Courtesy of the Glenbow Museum and Archives, NA 360-21

Victoria Belcourt Callihoo: Courtesy of the Lac Ste Anne Historical Society

Annie Laurie Robertson: Courtesy of the Glenbow Museum and Archives, NA 2750-36

William Griesbach: Courtesy of the City of Edmonton Archives, EA-10-1545

Cree family in Edmonton: Courtesy of the Provincial Archives of Alberta, B3

Ukrainian kids: Courtesy of the Provincial Archives of Alberta, B10464

Grace Duggan Cook: Courtesy of the University of Alberta Archives, 69-90

Alfred Bramley-Moore: Courtesy of Gladys Bramley-Moore, private collection

Peace and Norah Cornwall and friend: Courtesy of the Provincial Archives of Alberta, A-3806

Odilé David Samwald: Courtesy of Odilé David Samwald, private collection

Peter Owen: Courtesy of the Jewish Archives and Historical Society of Edmonton and Northern Alberta, with the permission of Peter Owen.

Bob Davies: Courtesy of Bob Davies, private collection

Johnny Bucyk: Courtesy of the Boston Bruins, National Hockey League

Chocolate Bar War: Courtesy of the City of Edmonton Archives, EA-600-42A

Karen Bower: Courtesy of Karen Bower, private collection

Kathleen Alexis: Courtesy of Kathleen Alexis, private collection

James Reininger: Courtesy of James Reininger, private collection

Angela Buteau: Courtesy of Angela Buteau, private collection

Jwamer Barzanji: Courtesy of Jwamer Barzanji, with the permission of Sabah Tahir and Jalal Barzanji, private collection

Bradley Pham: Ruth Linka, Brindle & Glass, with the permission of Sang and Ha Pham

Can you speak Kidmontonian?

Kids in Edmonton speak all of the languages of the world. The kids in this book speak many languages other than English. Here's a short list of new words in the stories.

Cree
Amiskwaciwâskihikan   *Beaver Hills House, the Cree name for Edmonton*
awâsisak   *children*
ayikîpîsim   *the frog moon, April*
misisâhkwak   *horseflies*
nehiyawak   *Cree people*
tân'si   *hello*

Blackfoot
nitsitapii   *the people, the name the Blackfoot people call themselves*

Nakoda
Aba Tã   *a very special day, like the pilgrimage or Easter*
moso macashdahwan   *I might go swimming*
Ti Oda   *Many Houses, the Nakoda name for Edmonton or Fort Edmonton*
Wakã mne   *God's Lake, the Nakoda name for Lac Ste. Anne*

French
bonjour   *hello*
votre petit garçon   *your little boy*

Ukrainian
dobry den   *hello*

German

auf wiedersehen   *goodbye*

Kurdish

topane   *soccer*

Vietnamese

đây là một thành phô rât tôt và đồng bào ơ đây cu̓ng rât tôt   *this is a nice place with nice people*

Hebrew

bar mitzvah   *a growing-up ceremony for Jewish boys who are thirteen years old. The ceremony for girls is called a bat mitzvah.*

Old-fashioned English words

aeroplanes   *the first spelling for airplanes; earlier they were called flying machines.*

automobiles   *the first word for cars, shortened sometimes to autos.*

bannock   *a tasty biscuit, often made in a frying pan over a campfire; popular among the Cree, Métis, and Scottish and French-Canadian pioneers. The Cree word for bannock is* pahkwesikan

barrel staves   *the curved wooden part of a barrel*

Beelzebub   *another name for a devil*

blunderbuss   *a gun used long ago*

chief factor   *the boss at a Hudson's Bay Company trading post*

coasting   *the old word for sledding or tobogganing*

conductor   *the driver of the streetcar*

hijinks   *mischief*

hobo   *a traveller without much money; sometimes a homeless person.*

muff   *a large fur mitt, open at both ends to keep both hands warm, worn by Canadian girls in winter; often made of rabbit fur* ninny   *a foolish person*

North West Mounted Police   *The first name for Canada's national police force. The name changed later to the Royal Canadian Mounted Police, but most people say RCMP or Mounties for short.*

pranksters   *kids who enjoy shenanigans, tomfoolery, and hijinks*

Red River cart   *a two-wheeled cart, pulled by a horse or pony, named for the nineteenth-century Métis community that grew into Winnipeg. The Red River cart was used on the plains and around Fort Edmonton in the late 1800s.*

Rupert's Land   *The Cree, Nakoda, and Métis people had their own names for every corner of the western plains when the English and French traders set up the first trading posts here in 1795. Canada wasn't a country yet. Until 1869, the English traders of the Hudson's Bay Company used the name Rupert's Land to describe the area we now know as Alberta, Saskatchewan, the Northwest Territories, Nunavut, Manitoba, and northern Ontario and Quebec.*

the scruff of the collar   *the back of the shirt*

shenanigans   *more mischief*

shinny   *A hockey game played for the fun of it at an outdoor rink, or on a frozen river, creek, or pond. Anybody who turns up can play.*

soap box derby   *a kids' race with homemade cars, very popular in the 1940s and 1950s. Edmonton's kids loved the soap box derby on McDougall Hill because of the curves in the road.*

streetcar   *an old-fashioned train that ran on tracks, and took passengers down streets and avenues, like the LRT. Buses replaced streetcars in the 1950s.*

tomfoolery   *even more mischief*

Acknowledgments

Many storytellers worked with me to adapt their life stories for this book. I appreciate their imagination and their generous assistance.

Kidmonton is one aspect of the *Edmonton: A City Called Home* project, an exploration of urban history that became the city's education project for the 2004 centennial with the encouragement of Mayor Bill Smith.

The Edmonton Public Library—the best friend of Edmonton's kids—is the headquarters of the project. I would like to thank Linda Cook, Director of Libraries; Keith Turnbull, the former associate director; and their colleagues at the EPL. Alva Shewchuk and the Education 2004 committee supported the project in the community, as did Jacqueline Broverman of Capital City Savings and Credit Union. The dedicated staff at the City of Edmonton Archives provided excellent research assistance.

I am grateful for the creative energy and commitment of Ruth Linka and Lee Shedden of Brindle & Glass Publishing, illustrator Rob Nichols, and researcher Carolina Jakeway Roemmich.

I owe Allan Shute a tip of the hat for coining the word 'Kidmonton' for an excellent city guidebook *Kidmonton: A Guide for Edmonton's Kids*, published by Tree Frog Press in 1978. His word deserved to be used again. I would also like to thank Nakoda Sioux linguist Eugene Alexis for his help with Nakoda Sioux words in the story; my reference for Cree words and expressions was the *Alberta Elders' Cree Dictionary*, by Nancy LeClaire, George Cardinal and Earle Waugh

Finally I would like to thank the smart, interesting kids in Janice Modesti's Grade 3-4 class at Riverdale Elementary School for their help and encouragement. They asked for a chapter book about Edmonton's history that was not too babyish and not too boring, a book without grownups in it. I hope I've delivered the goods.

LINDA GOYETTE is an Edmonton writer with an interest in Canadian history. A frequent contributor to Canadian magazines, she wrote for the *Edmonton Journal* for twenty years as a reporter, editorial writer, and editorial page columnist. She has won two National Newspaper Awards and a National Magazine Award for her writing.